Foreword by Lawrence Ray Park

SUCCESS IN BEAUTY

THE SECRETS TO EFFORTLESS FULFILLMENT AND HAPPINESS

COMPILED BY CHARLOTTE HOWARD
WOMEN LIFE MENTOR, AWARD-WINNING HAIR ARTIST, 5X'S BEST SELLING AUTHOR

Charlotte Howard - Heart Centered Women Publishing

1184 Old Mill Rd

Saint Stephen, SC/USA 29479

www.thehairartistassociation.org

charlotte@thehairartistassociation.org

Book Cover ©2014 Charlotte Howard - Heart Centered Women Publishing

Book Layout ©2014 Charlotte Howard - Heart Centered Women Publishing

Ordering Information:

Quantity sales. Special discounts are available on quantity purchases by corporations, associations, and others. For details, contact the "Special Sales Department" at the address above.

Success In Beauty: The Secrets To Effortless Fulfillment and Happiness Charlotte Howard. —1st ed.

ISBN-13: 978-0692310830

CONTENTS

DEDICATION

This book is dedicated to all of the women who desire to create what they want in life. That's YOU! Yes YOU!! It is my hope that this book empowers you to be more inspired, more confident and ready to take immediate action on pursuing and achieving your ideal goals, passions and dreams.

Wishing YOU love, peace and happiness!!

Charlotte Howard
Compiler of Success In Beauty

APPRECIATION

I'm grateful to god for all that he continues to do for me without him I do not know where I would be today. I'm grateful for my family and friends for being supportive and a very special thanks to my amazing kids Daija Howard, Daivontae Howard, Destiny Howard and Da'Kari Howard for being so understanding while mom continued to do all of her personal, business and life projects. I want to thank all of my mentors Ann Sieg, Pam Perry and Michael Cooch, who have really made a huge difference in my life.

I want to also thank all of my sister coauthors who have truly touched my heart and soul: Lisa Marie Rosati, Dr. Karen Jacobson, Cindy Christi, Elinor Stutz, Renee Dabney, Tina Hobson, Brenni Larson, Kellie R. Stone, Darlene Alexander, Sirena Pellarolo, Michelle Elizabeth, Marianne Chalmers Talkovski, Diane Aiello, Dr. Christina Kovalik, Bridgette Collins, Bonnie Bonadeo, Anni Diamond, Fawn Cheng and Anita Sechesky. I want to thank my team and success partners for helping us make a difference in the lives of women.

Finally I want to thank YOU for purchasing Success In Beauty: The Secrets To Effortless Fulfillment and Happiness. It is my mission to empower millions of women and it is because of women like YOU that my sister coauthors and I are now even closer to reaching our goal.

With Love,

Charlotte Howard
Compiler of Success In Beauty

FOREWORD

"There is nothing greater in this world than your burning desire and nothing more devastating in this world than to ignore it."-Lawrence Ray Parker

My position in the beauty industry was inherited - passed down like Elijah's mantel to Elisha when he transcended into the wind. Granny passed her mantle of beauty and business to me, before her battle with cancer carried her home. I will never forget that day.

Already a sophomore in high school, I remember my dad picking me up early, so that we could travel to Virginia to meet my mom, who was by her mother's side. What normally felt like an endless road trip from New Jersey to Virginia was over in the blink of an eye. Suddenly, we were at the hospital. Standing just outside her door, my entire family was crammed into her room. Staring at her weak and almost lifeless body, we knew it was time.

Without a second thought, I walked into the room and took command. I asked all the family to stretch their hands towards Granny and pray while I anointed her head and hands with blessed oil. My Granny, Marie S. Jordan, was a proud woman of God and strong in her faith. It felt like each touch to her head and body seemed to make her moan with relief, not pain. Was she releasing her gifts to me? Not 100% sure but things were never the same after that.

I was blessed to be the second eldest grandson to two amazing grandmothers. These talented women, one a hairstylist, the other a seamstress serviced the affluent women of the Greater Tidewater area. Granny, commonly called by her maiden name, Strong, always seemed to have a clump of blue magic on the back of her hand, giving those ladies a fresh press and shiny curls that would snap back for days.

These same women, first ladies to prominent preachers and college presidents, would be at my paternal grandmother, Willetta "Ms. Willie" Parker's house, for a fitting. Grandma (Willetta) and Granny (Marie) were amazing women who were damn good at their professions. Additionally, both had husbands, seven children a piece, lived in large homes and owned land. In fact, Granny bought each of her children a home before they were old enough to live in them alone. As a child, I did not know what all of this meant, but knew that I wanted the prosperity they had achieved.

Watching my grandmothers do what they loved was my gift. By the age of 13, I began thinking that I could do what they did. So I began my assent up the tree of beauty and insecurities. Though each branch represented a mastery of another skill, judgment from others accompanied my climb as well.

Sometimes, I worried what my father or other men would say about my interest in the beauty business, but my desire to keep learning drowned out the negativity. Thank God I persevered and answered my calling. Plus, I was hooked and this burning desire to do hair was greater than my fear of their judgment. Luckily, the examples set by my grandmothers and words of confirmation from my parents that I could have, do or be whatever I wanted to, was all I needed.

Their words were my foundation and my secret weapon when circumstances seemed unbearable or impossible.

Along my journey to excellence in the beauty business, I have learned that becoming a hairstylist is easy. Becoming a good businessman, however, is a much harder task. Too often people get hooked into this industry, hair or make up, just for the thrill of the finished look and forget to be professional or maximize their earnings. This is due to a lack of good business techniques. Believe it or not, even a minimum amount of service diversification will make a world of difference on many levels.

For instance, a licensed professional who supplies resale products for his/her clientele has many advantages. The client benefits from having needed products suggested to them by their own licensed stylist and made available to him/her without having to travel further to get it.

The client most likely would have purchased somewhere else anyway, but without the advice or referral from their licensed stylist. This would help prevent the client from shopping blindly and potentially purchasing inferior products. The stylist benefits in a number of ways as well. Having product available opens another stream of income and invites a new stream of non-service customers who will come to know you as a beauty supply as well as a salon. In other words, a stylist must think outside the box when it comes to creating multiple streams of income and not depend solely on providing one service to make a living.

There are countless fulfillment and happiness experiences offered in this book that will expand your business acumen and hopefully will unlock a burning desire within you. Use them. Let your own creative genius be stimulated by learning from others. I cannot imagine where I would be without the influences and examples of so many that came across my path and before me.

Lastly, while styling hair on a tv show taping in Alabama, I used the mornings to take walks along the beaches of the Gulf Coast. With the wind opposing me, each step seemed harder than the one before it.

Instead of turning back, I began walking in the steps that stretched out before me. My legs were relieved and it hit me that the experiences, decisions and perspectives of those who came before could be helpful on the path to obtaining my desires. That's what I learned from my grandmothers. And while you create your own footprints as you are pursuing your passions and dreams, give thanks and respect to those who came before you. Your success depends on it.

Anita Sechesky

Anita is a Registered Nurse, Certified Life Coach, International Best Selling Author x 3, Speaker, Trainer, Publisher, NLP and LOA Wealth Practitioner, as well as Big Vision Consultant. She is the CEO and Owner of Anita Sechesky - Living Without Limitations. Anita has assisted many people breaking through their own limiting beliefs in life and business. She has two International Best Sellers and is launching her first solo book "Absolutely You – Overcome False Limitations and Reach Your Full Potential" in November 2014. As a professional compiler and publisher, Anita can help you to put your passion on paper.

http://AnitaSechesky.com

https://www.facebook.com/asechesky

http://ca.linkedin.com/pub/anita-sechesky/3b/111/8b9

BEAUTIFUL THOUGHTS ARE CREATING MY BEAUTIFUL LIFE BY ANITA SECHESKY

When I was a young girl growing up in North-western Ontario, I often daydreamed of what it would be like if I looked like my favourite doll. There she was, just cruising along on the television commercials. All my friends loved her and her entire collection. It was a well-known fact how perfect my little doll was because every girl I knew who owned and played with her was quite excited to have all of her accessories and entourage. I didn't even have blonde hair, but it didn't matter to me. I couldn't believe how much a small plastic doll was loved by all the girls! I just knew it was something big when everyone loves and adores you.

Amazingly, this was one of those major defining moments in my young life because I can honestly say now as I look back I can see where I had started to apply the art of visualization, as technical as this may seem. Many people don't even realize that they are already applying it in their lives. This type of re-framing and concise perspective is a powerful method that I have used as a professional.

I have applied this tool to guide my own clients when they have faced challenges in their lives in order to not be discouraged, set goals, shift mind-sets, and achieve success. Yes, I admit it was a whole different aspect of observing my world when I was a child with limited life experiences to glean from, and yet it was the profound "doll" experience that helped me develop a positive mind-set.

Amazingly enough at such a young and impressionable age, and without the influence of others, that I made the decision of what I wanted in my life and I choose to focus on it until I achieved it. This was such a strong mind-set which I adapted into my persona that nothing which affected me negatively held me back anymore. I knew what it felt like to not really fit into the right groups and to see all the other popular kids doing their own thing together.

All that mattered at the time was that I had something to hold onto and pull me through me when things weren't so beautiful. Enough though I was not the most popular girl in school and my physical comparison was quite opposite to my plastic doll, I trained my mind to not focus on those differences. By accepting this obvious fact, I only saw the beauty in my life. I changed a negative into a positive.

I'm an eternal optimist even though I've experienced situations that were not my greatest moments ever. In retrospect, I can see how the energy going to a particular circumstance was the determining factor of this observation. So basically, if I choose to accept that a past experience happened and it did not discourage me from my goals or did not de-value me as a person to the point of causing me to give up on myself, then it did not have to be categorized as my worst experience ever.

I choose to process my life events into certain categories. I have adopted this strategy for quite some time, it's been working very effectively, and I can see how far I have come in such a short period of time. The place where I am in life right now has been a continual work in progress. It is not pit stop or even a bus stop. I may not have all the answers of how and what I am going to do about anything. I have now been through many experiences working as a Registered Nurse and as the compiler, visionary, and main author of the Living Without Limitations book series.

I thought I knew almost everything about human behaviour until I learned more about myself. I appreciate the simple fact that if things turn out a certain way, I choose not to stress over it more than I have to. This is quite challenging to do if you have nurturing qualities and are the fixer-up type. One of the greatest lessons I learned was when I understood within my spirit that I cannot change another human being from being themselves no matter how wrong they may be. It's not my place to even try. We all make choices and the consequences that result depend on our actions and reactions.

One way to think about this is how we can beautify the situation into something good. I always look for that glimmer of hope when things seem impossible – that there are no challenges, only opportunities to achieve something better than where I am at this moment. I have always chosen to have beautiful thoughts to create my beautiful life despite what my reality may actually be. I'm the type of person that does not like to focus on any negative thing in my life. My conviction for living this way is so strong. I disliked algebra very much in High School and I didn't give it the attention I should have, so when I was faced with algebra in my Nursing Program, I was required to pass with a mark of 90%.

In a short time, I quickly overcame my strong negative mind-set to embracing the fact that "I suddenly loved math." I loved it so much because I wanted to be an R.N. I recall meeting one of my former High School counselors at a community event. I told him that I was pursuing a career in nursing and his short sarcastic response was to laugh and wish me "Good luck!" I passed the course and I proved to myself and others that nothing is impossible when you choose to believe in yourself and your goals.

For me personally, I have always chosen to be optimistic and to not follow the crowd, meaning that if someone didn't like me or something about me, I chose never to become resentful or behave the way they did. Looking back now, I can see that my mom was my voice of reason, encouraging me to let go of any emotional upsets or hurts caused by others.

So instead of becoming angry and bitter, she encouraged me to choose forgiveness. As frustrating as it was for me as a young woman growing up, I realized that forgiveness was the healthier and sound-minded approach in life. I have gone through many experiences that weren't fair and if I had allowed myself to react from that place of offence or bitterness, it certainly wouldn't have been such a beautiful outcome.

17

Through some of these life events, I learned that people who wilfully disrespect and hurt others are more messed up and so caught up in their own issues that they have no understanding of the negative impact they are making on those around them. We are all responsible for our attitudes and behaviors. We must choose to cultivate a life of gratitude and love towards others. Each and every action and reaction is setting a tone for what life will give us back. I have learned to personally choose my thoughts and emotions towards others carefully. Having my feelings hurt is not a choice in life, but I have discovered that the negative energy associated with bad experiences and people is not a healthy way of living. It will draw you into a dark and demeaning life where you cannot see the blessings waiting for you because you can only focus on the offense. In doing so, the stress becomes compounded resulting in attracting more of the same nonsense. Why would I want that for myself?

Life already has its challenges and because we interact with so many individuals, why focus only on certain people when we have a whole world full of amazing souls waiting to be connected to us. As for me, Success in Beauty means that I have made a choice to focus on my beautiful thoughts in order to achieve the beautiful life I desire. I have always done so and although life is not perfect, it's how you choose to see it. I have walked through many unbelievable life events where others have tried to wilfully destroy or damage my dreams. But I have never allowed anyone to have that much power and control over my God-given destiny. When you have a dream that guides you into something bigger than yourself, life becomes more that just an opportunity to achieve things. It becomes a deeper spiritual and emotional connection to something greater than yourself. I strongly believe that we are all connected on a very deep and emotional level. Our lives have value and living in truth requires us to see the beauty in everyone and everything around us. The friction that takes places occasionally should never distract us from our higher calling and purpose as we position ourselves for greatness. We should be able to see the beauty and merit in those around us. Truly we are a reflection of love if we choose to believe.

Anni Diamond

Key note speaker, Transformational Success Coach and business owner, Author, Wife and Mother

After many requests from other business owners Anni decided to share her talents, her Intellectual Capital and her incredible savvy by packaging her formula that puts you in control of your business and your success. She runs masterclasses and has an online educational programme.

Anni is The Life Preneur expert who continues to change the lives of women with a No BS APPROACH to encouraging women to take charge of their lives by taking 100% responsibility for their actions and inactions.

Anni can help you discover that "YOU" are the solution.

www.beautysaloncoach.biz

www.spasalondivas.com

CANCER WAS MY GIFT BY ANNI DIAMOND

I've had an amazing life. I've had lots of money and opulence and lost it, made lots of money again and lost it again and clawing my way back up yet again. What have I learned? I've learned to work smart, to leverage my time and income. If you just trade hours for money, you have a ceiling or a limit to what you can earn. I've learned to create products that I can sell online, so I make money while I sleep.

I've learned to be gracious and look for the lessons everywhere. I've learned that you CAN teach an old dog new tricks. You just need to be open. You need to be open to change and willing to do the work. It's not in the knowing, it's in the DOING. It's taken me many years to understand that all I have created in my life was of my own doing, both good and bad.

Life has thrown me many curve balls over the years. Like most women, we believe we have to be perfect at everything we do. Wife, mother, career, lover, and business owner. Well perfection doesn't exist. It's a myth. You know that. I know that. It's a lie handed down from generation to generation, for what purpose I don't know.

You've heard the expression practice makes perfect, and perfect practice makes perfect. I say bollocks. I say "just start". Don't wait for perfection before you get going. Just get going and learn along the way. Just move forward in the direction of your goals and dreams and watch them appear one by one in front of your eyes as you work daily towards them.

Have you heard of the Rule of 5? Well this simply means you do 5 things every day to get your closer to your destination, your goal or your dream. If you set your internal GPS and work with the Rule of 5, you will get closer to your pay day every day.

In 2013, I had a small business that was doing very well in the beauty industry. I've been the sole provider for the last 16 years as my husband had an accident that left him with an acquired brain injury in 1999. It hasn't been an easy road.

In October I decided to move the clinic into larger premises so I was preparing for the move. At the same time, my husband was diagnosed with dementure. I was just processing the devastating news. 4 weeks later we did the clinic move on November 5th, 2013. On November 21st I was diagnosed with cancer. My whole world turned upside down.

How could this be happening to me? I can't get sick, I've got a husband with a disability, a business, kids and people that rely on me every day for their income.

Well, cancer doesn't wait for anyone to get their affairs in order. I had my first surgery that same day, my next surgery on December 10th, my next surgery on January 6th and my next surgery on April 20th. I had chemotherapy every second week. I would be in hospital for three days every fortnight. I had a bag full of chemo that I carried around in a bum bag.

Very fashionista. All the while sick as a dog. I was so exhausted. I would drive an hour to work every day and an hour home. I was so sick, most days I didn't even know how I got to work or home. I don't think I was a great leader at this time, but my business still needed a captain of the ship. I was on overwhelmed mode.

I stood doing some ironing one particular morning and I was trapped in my own head. I wasn't thinking about dying, or pain or anything like that. I was thinking about my business. I just didn't want to go to work anymore. I wanted to feel sorry for myself and have some time to myself without the stresses of life. Good luck with that one!

Anyway, then once again my logic kicks in and I ask myself how can I keep the business making money and get myself well at the same time. I'm not asking myself how did I cause this, but rather what causes this? I believe that I have been under so much stress for so long, that it causes toxicity in the body which in turn causes inflammation in the cells which in turn causes disease. This might not be an accurate portrayal of toxicity and inflammation, but I'm sure you get where I'm going with this.

So many people rely on me every day. How am I going to change this? How did I set this up in the first place, I ask myself?

I was meant to have 12 rounds of chemo, but after 4 rounds, I thought I was going to die from the drugs. To everyone's surprise I stopped having the treatment. I found a biochemist to work with, a great naturopath, I bought an infra-red detox sauna and an oxygen concentrator.

Cancer was a gift. It has made me make changes in my life. I'm trying really hard to remove the stress of business. I'm not quite there yet, but I have a plan that I work towards everyday using the Rule of 5, to get me closer to where I want to be.

"My strength didn't come from lifting weights... My strength came from lifting myself up again when I got knocked down.....
"
I want to share an excerpt from my personal diary with you.

"Ok now it's Saturday and I'm all alone in the old shop, still cleaning out and taking bits and pieces to the new shop. Today I'm feeling beaten, defeated. I feel like I want to throw my hands in the air and giving up. Just let someone look after me for a while.

Where's my soft place to fall. Don't have one. I'm it. Remember that my husband has an acquired brain injury and he is trying his best to help, but what I truly need is someone to talk to, someone to download to, so you are it today. I was beginning to feel vulnerable. I want to get off this merry go round. I had a sh… client yesterday afternoon, who just got to me. Like you, I'm sure you take it personally and it's hard to shake the crap off. I'm sick to my stomach today.

I'm trying really hard to get my head back in the right place today but I'm really struggling." Why am I sharing this with you? Because I'm human, I'm just like you. I have good days and bad days. There are days I want to give up. What keeps me going? Well I hope you read my first book so you have more of an understanding of what it takes to have success. The road is not easy. It's full of challenges and roadblocks.

There are many days that I want to quit. I want to curl up in a ball and have a big cry. Many days I'm over tired and overwhelmed. My husband is deteriorating, depressed and frustrated which adds another layer of overwhelm and frustration to me.

Now the tears are flowing while I'm typing. I want you to know that raw emotion is OK to share. It's OK to be vulnerable. It's ok to feel what you feel, but it's always how you deal with it that makes the difference and changes the ending to your story. Sometimes it's hard not to become the victim in your story and I think that it is OK to be the victim, but only for a minute. It's OK to feel sorry for yourself and have a sooky la la moment. But, it's not OK to wallow for very long in this black hole.

My point here is that even though there are times that I feel like sh…... I feel like giving up. I feel like I don't want to do "this" anymore……... and by "this" I mean life (I don't mean topping myself – lol), just mean , well you know, I mean the merry go round. Tomorrow will be another day, I'll dust myself off, think positive thoughts and move forward towards my new goals.

My point is that if I don't give up, if I don't quit, every day I'll move closer to my big payday. I've got a plan, a dream to set myself up. Winners don't quit and quitters don't win!

You get to write your own story in life. You can choose to be the victim or victorious. You get to be the heroine of your own story.

What's next for me? Well, I've just listed my business for sale. I need to learn to be whole and happy and NOT in survival mode. I need to find time for ME. I need to stop pushing to survive and just enjoy and surrender to what- ever is coming next. I know the best part of my life is still yet to come.

Big hugs
Anni Diamond

Bonnie Bonadeo

Bonnie Bonadeo - Arakara LLC, The Beauty Agents Speaker – Education Resource Company, Beauty Goorus Coaching & Consulting, and Co-founder of Naked Audience Productions. Bonnie has represented the beauty industry 25+ years by Connecting People to the Power of Beauty. Her experience in the industry started as a stylist, to managing salons, and working for some of the most notable manufacturers and distributors to directing the industry's most celebrated events. As a 2013 Enterprising Women and a certified Emotional Intelligent Speaker, Bonnie speaks on her struggles and successes as a leader and entrepreneur to foster growth and awareness in others.

www.bonniebonadeo.com

www.thebeautyagents.com

www.beautygoorus.com

www.napevents.com

"Success consists of going from failure to failure without a loss of enthusiasm." -Winston Churchill

BEAUTY ENTHUSIASM, MY JOURNEY TO JOY BY BONNIE BONADEO

After 25+ years in the beauty industry and many roles, I was always the cheerleader for enthusiasm, which was easy when it came to what other people were making, selling or offering. However, when it came to my stuff, enthusiasm was disguised as fear and a fight laced with, am I good enough, will I succeed, what if I fail, who would follow me and why?

Why was it I could support other people's ideas but fell flat when I had to believe and promote my own ideas? The story is always the same, the creative artist whose work or concept is never good enough to put out just yet as there is always something more to be done, fixed or recreated to make it perfect and for one reason only.... to avoid rejection. So I kept working for others that was enough.

In my many successes in beauty most of them came with the fight, you know the human protective behaviors we express when survival is at risk; fight, flight or freeze. Well I'm a fighter and I fought my way through all my so called successes. Then one day I was too tired to fight, I lost my passion I didn't believe in my ideas, it appeared neither did some of my so called followers, I scoffed at others ideas behind my breath. I went from this passionate influencer to a passionless introvert. Of course, that is what others called me "passionate", it was a nice way of saying I was too emotionally charged or overly excited when trying to get others to see my point of view! But I liked being an emotionally charged gal, I got stuff done with the old adage "sales is nothing more than a transfer of enthusiasm" and all of my J.O.B.s in sales, marketing and education were easy...I was good at it for someone else so how could I not be a success for me.

Finally, I started my own beauty businesses, not just one but two, an agency and a consulting company. All was going and growing, with hard work, enthusiasm and fighting to stay alive I made more as an entrepreneur in my first year than in my last job. Then one day (I am not sure when it happened) I lost my enthusiasm, I felt waves of exhaustion, betrayal, feelings of being beaten up and disregarded, I went from a fighter to frozen, who was I and why could I not put up my dukes and charge ahead like before... how did I lose my soul, my fire, my passion and how do I get it back?

More work, more training more education that was always my answer....and I became a certified emotional intelligent leader and co-founded another company based on authentic communications to teach others how to become their authentic self through speaking, leading and selling. Yes, I was getting my passion back and in a newfound way, through mastering the art of authentic connection. Only to realize that as the teacher I became the student of authentic transformation and it was painful.

Starting another company was like going from one child to two, it was not easier it's just more work, but you have learned the lessons on what you can skip with the new one. So if starting another company was going to be more work, I felt I could do it, but it paled in comparison to starting the new me! I discovered, I was just adding things to the outside of me to find success and still not creating it from within. I struggled with myself, I could literally feel layers of the old me slipping away and me hanging on to them for reasons to exist, this transformation I was going through had me in tears, in bed for days and unable to coexist with the special people in my life. Undoubtedly some of those people went away as if they never existed in my life to begin with. I didn't feel success; I felt loss and betrayal not only with others but with me. It was easy to be something for someone else but when you have to be you for you...do you know who U are?

My coaches and qualified confidants all said the same thing; you are using work to avoid finding the real you... maybe it's time to finally just BE U? BE U, I don't know who this U is and I am not sure I like her, she seems passive, not the leader and go getter like before. However, all of their conversations were powerfully convincing. "Aren't you exhausted by the fight, don't you believe there is another and easier way of being successful and joyful." I heard the word not easier or successful but joyful, who's joyful what does that word really mean and how do I get some of that. Is it another word for passion or enthusiasm...? Is it possible to be truly joyful? I knew that because I did not possess this emotion called joy that there was no going back to who I was and only moving forward to find this elicit thing called joy and so my journey begins to find, embrace and enthusiastically own joy.

I knew I had to find the joy within me to really claim it, and wondered is joy our connection with BEing U? I thought about getting another dog and calling it Joy so it gave me a reason to use the word but that would have been transferring the responsibility to someone or something else, this was internal not external. So I made a list of things that I believed created joy for me? It wasn't a long list and consisted of the usual, family, friends, animals, hiking, traveling the world, writing and speaking, defined as teaching, training, creating programs, having a voice and being heard, powerfully being heard. Not because I am angry or need to be right but because I do have something to share and I am good at transferring information and relevancy to topics, subjects and ideas for others to grow from. I knew it was time to let go of my ego related to success and create opportunities for me to express my emotions, authentically own my passion for writing and public speaking and find my joy.

As I was discovering my new self and my new joy, I was very emotional, more like emotionally unstable and went through months feeling groundless, uncertain and insecure. . . there was nothing wrong with me other than my failure to accept that the old me had no reason to exist and to gracefully and lovingly let her go as my BEaUtiful authentic self began to get exposed through the cocoon. Being this vulnerable brought up so many fears and past experiences all I could think was that I was failing.

Although, I felt I was on the right path I was determined to see the BEaUty in life...my life without the fight but "what you resist persists". My failure to accept not fighting had me in the fight of fighting more. Not with others but with me the inward fight not the outward fight. It threatened my life, my business and my existence and this time I needed to listen. I began to fail forward and I now understand that feeling groundless and uncertain is allowing vulnerability to be present. I learned to speak my naked truth and the art of saying no. This was a BEaUtiful revelation. My journey to BE was unveiling, naked and inevitable because there is no one else to BE but me. I was I so determined to please everyone else in my life that what looked like failure was actually my Be U finally emerging. The growing pains of being my own version of success and knowing what my contributions are to others have become my new journey... failures, flaws and all.

It seems as we grow and evolve we can choose to struggle or we can transform. We can choose to chase success or authentically allow our contribution to be bestowed to others. Transformation of self and finding that moment when you can say I am really, truly and honestly comfortable in my own skin is when you have found that place of joy. I have found that place of joy and how lucky am I that I get to share these stories, and journeys with the others in beauty. I know that the beauty within me is me and finding the BEaUty within U cannot be a success if you fail to release what holds you back. Don't fight BEing U, know that you are a contribution and express the BEaUty Enthusiasm that emanates in you so you too can share and provide joy for others.

Brenni Larson

Brenni Larson is best known as the "Feng Shui Messenger" with almost 200 hours of interviews with Feng Shui specialists. November of 2012, she created and hosted the "Feng Shui Messenger Academy", interviewing Feng Shui specialists. Listeners were given immediate action steps to enhance the energy of their environment.

By applying the tools of Feng Shui, the listeners are able to clear their energy, thus raising the vibration of their space. As you vibrate at a higher frequency, you attract like vibration. "Attention to it, Puts it on Your Plate…Abraham-Hicks"

Recently Brenni expanded into the holistic and spiritual world, gather specialist and the community, to assist her with her mission. With a background in many healing modalities, from Native American influence, to dream teacher, oracle card reader, light and grid work, Angels and Ascended Masters to Resonance Re-patterning, the universe was insisting she share it all.

Join Brenni on her mission to reach over 9 million that are in the "flow" to raise the vibration of planet!

Contact Information:

Brenni@brenni-larson.com

218 -270 -8117

THE JOURNEY TO YOUR SOUL'S PURPOSE BY BRENNI LARSON

Whose Life are YOU Living? Is it yours? Are you happy living a life that is a mold designed by your family, teachers, and society? They did what they thought was right, but you know there is something missing, or not in balance in your life.

If you are confused about why you are here, what your purpose or mission is … let me ask you this simple question.

Are you LIVING A LIFE of JOY and EXPANSION?

If not, you are not living YOUR SOUL'S PURPOSE! But, you already know this, or you wouldn't be searching for something to make you feel comfortable with who you are. You wouldn't continue looking for teachers, and others you can relate to.

You wouldn't keep trying to find YOU… because you already know deep inside the REAL YOU! YOU KNOW what makes you happy, where you find joy… if all you had to do was LIVE… what LIFE would you DREAM? That is your DESTINATION point … the starting point is NOW!

It is easy. You can feel it. You KNOW DEEP INSIDE if you are on track with the mission of your soul…. Your chakras are the guidance system and is always communicating through your emotions.

Feel the energy in your body. Follow you "gut" feeling… that is your solar plexus, your "sun center" your "power center" guiding you!

Do you wake up each morning with a joy and excitement about day ahead of you? Are you happy? Are you making a contribution to the world?

If you answered yes, keep doing what you are doing … if not, then read on… and may the "chaos to clarity" of my journey help you to get to your destination with less turbulence and your landing be smooth. But first….

Calm and Center Yourself [do this exercise 3 times slowly]:
• Sit in nature, or a place that is quiet and comfortable
• Close your eyes
• Listen only to nature or your breath
• Now, take a deep breath in through your nose to your
• Lower belly
• Middle belly
• Lungs
• Hold for a count of three
• Release through your mouth, with a big sigh
• Visualize all stuck energy leaving your body
• Each breath in is filling your body with clean, fresh fuel for you

Below is my story. The ups and downs and aha moments, on the journey back to ME…   My writing is to empower you, through example, to live the life YOU are HERE to LIVE! YOU living your mission, is a piece of the puzzle of life… the YOU that is here to make a difference on this planet!

My family said I was born with a mind of my own, and trouble from the start. Mom said, "When the nurse handed you to me, I knew you were going to be trouble by the way you looked at me!" So, within a few minutes of being born, I was given my first label "trouble" …. a label that would follow me my entire life.

Before I was 4 years old, I knew I didn't fit the "mold" that was poured for me by my family and society. Being the opposite of my sister, I can hear my parents say "why aren't you more like your sister?"

What? Why would I want to be someone else? It didn't make any sense to me. I rolled my eyes, and told them "I love me! That's not nice to say that!", and stomped off and escaped in nature.

As I grew, so did the labels assigned to me. The more I was told I wasn't supposed to be me, the more my natural personality took over. Nature has always been an escape, a big play ground, and living in the country, I was always off participating in the energy of life in the woods.

My family saw the gifts of my personality as negative, and instead of nurturing these wonderful God given qualities, they created "guilt and shame" around my uniqueness.

Part of being labeled, is being raised in a German – Catholic family. One of the toughest barriers for me, was to let go of feeling guilty. Guilt is a low vibrating energy, and God / Universe doesn't play that tune!

It is great to be unique! You are dancing to your song, your music! We all have a part to play in the story life. Why not enjoy the ride, and have fun! Set your mind to that right now!

Life seemed so simple as a child. As soon as I opened my eyes, I smiled with excitement for the day. Nature was full of activity, and my imagination painted the mystical journey that was awaiting for me. No one needed to tell me I loved nature, cloud watching, star gazing, swimming, biking, or comfortable clothes. It came easy, because I was BE-ing me.

Full of LIFE and JOY and EXPANSION, is how I came into this world. It was the energy that existed when I took my first breath. I learned this later, in Feng Shui… I am exactly the Brenni that God intended me to be.

My BIG energy and thunderous voice didn't take long for me to be labeled "motor mouth" "energizer bunny" "trouble maker", and I was blamed for everything. It used to get me very upset and angry when they wouldn't stop. I would stomp my foot and respond with my "thunderous" voice. This would continue until I left in tears, and then they would laugh and call me cry baby.

Later on, after many lessons, I found the road to Feng Shui, which validated I was the me I was supposed to be. The 5 elements and the flow of Yin and Yang, explained why I was attracted, or attracted certain people and situations in my life.

On the journey, when one of my Feng Shui mentors explained my "4 Pillars of Destiny" and Ming Gua [my personal energy that existed the second I took my first breath] to me, it validated that The ME I feel is the ME I am supposed to be!

Below is a short example, of my elemental traits, and how I discovered I am exactly … yes, down to the "Thunderous" voice that others try to change in my personality, is MY ENERGY!

The journey led me to my Ming Gua , my personal energy of 3 Wood East Life Group. It is the Family sector or Gua of the Bagua, and the Tri-gram is THUNDER. Below is the example of this means.

My element is 3 wood [young wood]. My energy is grass in the spring, and my mind is always creative and bursting with new ideas [like the seeds planted in the spring, pushing through the soil].

Water feeds Wood in the 5-elemental cycle. You water a plant or tree to nourish it. Fire burns up wood. So if wood out of balance is either being pushed over like a willow tree, or snap [anger – the emotion of wood] like dry wood.

I love being on or near lakes and water, and live in the country surrounded by nature and trees, [water and wood]. When I lived in Dallas, a big and busy [yang] city, I was out of balance. It was in the south [fire burns up wood] and I got more and more angry, and would snap at people.

Missing certain things in my chart {zero FIRE], and not knowing it as I was in my 20-40 year old span, I made poor choices [1/3 of Chinese Luck] and my surroundings [1/3 of Chinese Luck] set me up for distaster... 2/3 of my Luck... my Journey in life was out of balance!

1. [momentum moment - mm] is a creating movement forward.

Here is an example: In the beginning it may be hard to get a car "moving", but once you do, it is easier to continue to move forward. That is what we will accomplish in this chapter... creating momentum towards your Joy and Expansion, which is why I believe we are here.

Momentum Exercise: Release the Old, Lock in the New

Take blank recipe cards and write negative labels you feel you have. Give no energy or emotion to it. Write one word on each card. Burn the cards, with the intention you are releasing the labels from your grid. The smoke carries your wishes to Heaven.

[The most powerful time to perform is during a New Moon ceremony. Burn the cards between 11 pm and 1 am [1 hour of night (yin) 1 hour of day (yang).

2. Now, play some music and just dance and shake any way your "body moves you"... shake out the old... lock in the new!

3. Dream... act like you are a child, and with no filter. You can have anything you desire.

Get out of the "Why ME" right now... that is pity for yourself, and you will never move forward to complete your Soul's Journey. Stop. Breathe. Now inhale and relax. Each "challenge" or "obstacle in life is a road map or lesson learned, and you are closer to your Destination ... the Journey to Your Soul's Mission... Your Purpose ... Your Contribution...

Bridgette Collins

Fitness coach Bridgette L. Collins is the owner of Total Innovative Wellness Solutions, LLC, a consulting firm that provides individuals and organizations with strategic solutions for implementing and sustaining healthy lifestyle habits. Coach Collins is the author of three books, Broken In Plain Sight, Destined to Live Healthier: Mind, Body, and Soul, and Imagine Living Healthier: Mind, Body, and Soul. She is featured in The Ultimate Runner by Ultimate HCI Books, publisher of the Chicken Soup for the Soul series. Her story, "Never Give Up: My Journey to Become a Runner", of transitioning from the sofa to the streets to become a marathon runner has inspired many to move their lifestyle habits in a different direction.

Learn more about Coach Collins at www.BridgetteCollins.com. Don't forget to follow her on Twitter at www.twitter.com/askcoachcollins, friend her on Facebook at www.facebook.com/bridgettelcollins, and read her blog posts at www.askcoachcollinsblog.com.

THE IMPACT OF PAIN ON PURPOSE BY BRIDGETTE COLLINS

Looking back eleven years ago, I still remember vividly the pain and uncertainty that consumed every day of my life for nearly two years. In my mind during that time, I imagined the year 2003 as my breakout year for becoming a sought after health and fitness expert for both private and public sectors. God had already blessed me to be in a position to educate, inspire and empower others to live healthy, and I was so grateful for the opportunities coming my way, and I was even more proud that others considered me a creditable healthy living resource.

I was having a blast writing fitness articles for publications, conducting fitness seminars, running marathons and coaching marathon training programs. I was savoring a long overdue passion that made my life more meaningful and purposeful. So, yes I needed more than a few moments to absorb the painful state that surfaced and infiltrated my body later that year.

What started out as unprecedented coughing attacks were just the beginning of my ailments in early 2003. After nearly six weeks of unsuccessful resolutions which included using over the counter medications, I finally scheduled an office visit to see my general practitioner, Dr. Conard. Unsure of the root cause, he prescribed a combination of medications to treat symptoms associated with a cold, allergies, or respiratory tract illness. Just when the coughing attacks appeared to be under control, I was plagued by another setback a few weeks later.

I began to experience unmanageable bouts of itching all over my body. To combat the chain reaction of itching and scratching, I tried a series of over the counter anti-itching creams and lotions. I even tried bathing in lukewarm water with baking soda and oatmeal. None of which remedied my ailments!

Persistent itching throughout the day at work caused me to become self-conscious about my urges to scratch, and the subtle approaches to rub my itching arms, legs, back, and stomach areas felt awkward. Wondering if anyone noticed me stealing moments to scratch my thighs underneath the conference room table caused me much worry.

Because my job required constant contact with others, I often excused myself during meetings to go to the restroom to scratch relentlessly the various parts of my body. It was my hope that my private mass scratching efforts would taper the itching long enough for me to perform the functions of my job.

After the repeated failed attempts of relief, I scheduled an appointment to see Dr. Conard. On the day of my visit, Dr. Conard began to ask a series of questions.

"Where exactly do you itch?"
"Mainly on my hands, thighs, arms, back, and stomach and they leave red welts that look like bug bits."
"Are you on any medications that I'm not aware of?" he asked. "Some medications can cause itching.

Beyond an allergic reaction to a certain medication, someone who might also be taking prescription drugs such as diuretics can experience the effects of dry skin that can result in itching. Even beyond the constant itching can sometimes be signs of diseases such as kidney failure or diabetes or even cancer."

"No doctor, I'm not taking any medications. That is, other than the medications I was taking for the coughing."

After inquiring about the possibility of Eczema, Dr. Conard said, "You don't have Eczema. Although the look of Eczema differs from person to person, it is most often distinguished by dry, red, extremely itchy patches on the skin. Basically when you itch you rash." Minimal relief led Dr. Conard to refer me to an allergist and dermatologist for a variety of specialized tests.

Longing for a breakthrough, I prayed and prayed for relief. But, my trips to the allergist and dermatologist resulted in more and more out of pocket medical costs and even more confusion and worry.

Days later, Dr. Conard's office called me to schedule a visit. During my visit he informed me that the results of my blood work revealed high levels of protein in my urine and a severe low red blood cell count.

"What could be the reason for the high protein level and low red blood cell count?" "Reasons for the high levels of protein are usually associated with a kidney problem or it could be any number of other reasons like high blood pressure, acute allergic reaction, or Lupus," Dr. Conard said. "I'm going to refer you to a hematologist."

"What about my red welts? They come and go."

Dr. Conard proceeded to poke around my body and said, "Based on the information from your dermatologist, the red welts are known as Urticaria. A diagnosis of Uticaria which are hives is typically a result of an allergic reaction to food or medicine."

"According to the allergist, I did not have food allergies and I'm not on any sort of medication." "They also develop because of infection or illness related to emotional stress, extreme cold or sun exposure, excessive perspiration, all of which could pertain to you -- that is, because you participate in a sport that places stress on your body, places you in extreme weather conditions and causes excessive perspiration," he said.

At this point, I started to wonder if my love for running was the culprit. Just as I was trying to wrap my mind around the trail of ailments another one surfaced. Severe pain and swelling in my hands and joints emerged. As he considered all of the new ailments, Dr. Conard began the discussion about running tests for an autoimmune disorder and referring me to a rheumatologist. I knew the one thing I wasn't going to do was let Dr. Conard or some other doctor tell me I had a disease.

I knew I had to work hard at figuring out and implementing the activities I had control over to help me to get better. Above all, I knew a reliance on God was vital to my restoration. I kept Him as my focal point. And that focal point led me to do more and more research.

In August 2003 everything that had been building up culminated in the worse way. Awakening to a body under attack with an endless and indescribable pain, swelling and stiffness, I was unable to get out of bed due to my paralyzing state. Days after being bed-ridden, I was transported to the rheumatologist who after analyzing blood tests diagnosed and determined a treatment plan for inflammation running rampant throughout my body.

My rheumatologist's best description for what I was experiencing was 'Lupus-like' symptoms. Thereafter, I decided I needed something more extensive than the doctor's treatment plan and was led to embark upon a 40-day spiritual journey. By this time, I was under the care of a parade of doctors, my general practitioner, rheumatologist, dermatologist, and hematologist for the itching, pain, swelling and stiffness, skin hives and low red blood count.

With the improvements that resulted from my treatment plan came the forecasted side effects related to a rounded face, acne, hair loss and a twenty pound weight gain. But, it was okay. Even though my mobility was strained and my ability to perform my normal life activities was impaired, I was finally starting to feel better.

While on my spiritual journey, I realized that life is filled with unknowns and challenges and that no one is spared. It was my belief that God was waiting to see how I was going to respond to what He had allowed to happen to me.

It was God's test for me. It would have been easy to accept my rheumatologist's bleak forecast that I was on the verge of a Lupus diagnosis or that I might not ever run again, but it was my hope and belief that God had a greater plan and purpose for my life. With my hope, belief and prayer, and the support of family and friends and their hope, belief and prayers I dismissed what could have been accepted as shattering news.

Despite numerous set-backs, a year later I was able to resume a somewhat normal life. I will never forget the Thursday in September 2004 when my rheumatologist told me I was in remission. I knew it was nothing but God working His plan in my life so that I would find my true purpose. I am so grateful for that time in my life because it is when I learned the essence of faith, hope and prayer.

As I stated in my opening paragraph, I had imagined the year 2003 as my breakout year. But as He often does, God had a different plan. There were a lot of quiet times that I used to talk to Him. My connection to God is what kept my hope out front and my faith continued. If I had allowed worry, despair, frustration and fear to settle in my life, I know my outcome may have been a different one.

I know the pain I endured was necessary for me to realize my true potential and recognize my true purpose of delivering messages of hope, faith, and healing. God's plan included me training people with chronic health problems to run in endurance events and writing books to help the masses navigate their personal challenges to live healthier: mind, body and soul.

Cindy Christi

Cindy Christi produces inspiring content, pairs it with customized business models, irresistible calls to action and unique distribution platforms to attract world-class media alliances, sponsorships and positive change. As a media personality, producer and digital publisher who's passionate about making a difference, She serves by designing, funding, hosting, producing, and distributing content with a focus on positive transformation, personal discovery and global contribution.

If YOU make the world a better and more beautiful place, Cindy Christi wants to tell your story!

Here is a link to her Publisher's letter "Something Beautiful" in Get Image Ready Magazine's Inspiration Issue: http://issuu.com/getimageready/docs/inspiration_issue/2

A link to an interview where she shares how and why she gives back: http://issuu.com/getimageready/docs/inspiration_issue/18

And, a link to connect with her so she can become a part of YOUR success story: http://about.me/CindyChristi

GET IMAGE READY FOR ANY STAGE LOVE IT, LIVE IT, GIVE IT BY CINDY CHRISTI

Wait, Where's My Beauty Manual?

I looked up and thought, "WOW so that's what snowflakes look like!" Only these were dry, much bigger than I expected, and as they fluttered down from the ceiling right on queue, my job was to sing, look cute and act pleasantly surprised as the set was magically covered in snow. My co-stars and I had our day planned from early to late with rehearsals, wardrobe, catered meals, tutors, set changes and lots of laughs as we performed alongside comedian Rich Little for "The House that was Filled with Love" a World Vision's special shot at NBC Studios Burbank in the heart of Sunny California.

Guess what I wore? An adorable rainbow plaid jumpsuit, ruffled socks, pearls and a pair of pigtails. Oh yes, from the stages of Universal Studios to NBC to every kid's audition in Hollywood, I had "CUTE" down.

By the time I was nine, I was an actress, student and self-proclaimed producer. No Barbie dolls for me! I was creating and choreographing my own shows at home with my two sisters, our neighbor's kids, 27 chickens, cocker-poodle and dad's cam-corder. I LOVED the camera, the stage, and everything that had to do with the magical world of entertainment so much I even remember saying in one of my auditions that if they picked me I would be happy to do the job for *free*!

Little did I know that any money I made from bookings barely covered the expense of acting school, SAG-AFTRA dues or putting gas in my mom's car for my auditions or that it was a weekly sacrifice for my parents to just make ends meet. Lucky for me, they saw how happy I was and believed my manager when she told them I had what it took.

I was a nine-year-old ROCKSTAR on a roll who would have been happy doing what I was doing for the rest of my life.

Somewhere between the ages of 10 and 13 however, my "cute" jumpsuits, leg warmers and plastic jelly shoes were no longer cutting it in a world of bright neon, ripped jeans and mile high mullets…and making matters worse, bookings started to dwindle as I was now the girl with acne, long lanky limbs and buck-teeth.

For the first time, I was painfully aware that my image was in need of a serious overhaul or my budding career would be in danger. I knew I needed professional help!

Be Careful What You Wish For

I don't recall the school, but I do remember seeing beautiful girls my age framed on the walls as I walked in for my interview. My mom and I were brought into the office of a charismatic older gentleman with a 1960's Mad Men bouffant who asked a few questions about who I was and how I heard about their school. I shared that I learned about them through one of my friends at school who also happened to be one of the prettiest girls framed on their walls and was there to see if they could help me with my image.

He then proceeded to tell me about their very prestigious school. If accepted, I would learn dining etiquette, what to wear for my body type, how to clear up my acne and apply my make-up. I would also learn how to take the perfect photo, walk, sit, hold my shoulders, and how to wear my hair for every occasion. Listening to him, I sat a little taller, smiled a little larger and my heart swelled with happiness as I visualized how great I life would be once I was finally landing all my auditions again.

Touring the building, I pictured myself in every room learning from a team of experts on how to dress for the part I wanted most: the prettiest most confident version of ME so I could land the BIG roles, help my family and live my passion!

Believing that my image would play a significant role in fulfilling these aspirations, I knew that modeling school was my answer and I was READY.

To be honest, I don't remember how the interview ended. I don't even remember shaking the man's hand good-bye. I was so utterly shocked by what happened next, I simply blocked it out of my memory.

I was accepted to the school, but unbeknownst to me, financial pressures were mounting at home. My acting career was no longer paying for it self like it used to, and with needing to pay for braces, not only did my father say no to modeling school, he also decided it was time to put my dreams of acting on hold too!

What??? How long is "on-hold"? Until I was18? But I'm only 13! That's 5 Yeeeeears! I was shattered. Should I rally, bargain and plea? Should I go on strike? Should I run away? Should I ask my manager to take me in and live with her until I made it?

Of course the bigger questions loomed deep in my heart, without acting or modeling who was I? Did it matter anymore if I was pretty? And would my success ever be something I could control?

Although running away and going on strike was tempting for about a week, I chose the high road, stayed home and got good grades. Like most hard lessons, this experience would also change my perspectives in life for the better; I came to realize that outward beauty and appearances meant nothing without inner beauty and purpose and that my success was determined by my attitude, *not* the other way around.

Inspirational Productions

By 19 I was in community college and while driving back and forth to school and work, I started hearing radio commercials promoting Inspirational Production's upcoming National Talent Search. My mother heard them too, and encouraged my 2 sisters and I to audition.

As fate would have it, the 3 of us were accepted out of hundreds of applicants, and through an amazing sequence of events a secret sponsor offered to give me a full scholarship; a gift that would change my life.

It was as if God picked up all the broken pieces of my 13 year old heart and put them back together again. All the things I loved about acting and modeling were provided in a condensed format of talent, runway and competition workshops. Within a few short weeks we were "Agent Ready" for top Casting Directors and scouts from Arizona and California!

I won in my category, was signed with Ruth Leighton Agency and was invited to join them in Seattle and Century City as part of their production crew. We worked together, performed together, ate together, and we even PRAYED together. It was a new kind of beauty that touched my soul. Having not grown up in a Faith based environment (other than attending a few bible studies with friends), I was truly amazed to see this level of love expressed in the entertainment industry, on the road and in a hotel room.

When we returned at the end of summer, I attended a Church service in Scottsdale with the team where I was given a personal message of hope to stay the course, to know I was meant for media and to know that when the blessings came that they would come from God. I also realized that perhaps my dreams were not meant for me alone but for a calling that could make a difference. If my love for the camera, the stage and for story telling could be used to serve and bless others, then maybe *my life* would help to make the world just a little more beautiful!

Fast Forward

In the years that have followed those transformational moments, I've fulfilled many of the goals I set out for myself. Working as a media professional I've gone from being an on-air host to becoming an executive producer, to launching my own TV channel and co-developing global media initiatives for women and girls. That's not to say it's been an easy road, it hasn't, and I wouldn't have had it any other way. If anything, it's helped me understand the true value of giving back.

No one makes their journey alone and I am forever grateful to the mentors I've had along the way. In turn, I've realized that it's not only a privilege to give; it's a way to affirm my convictions. I believe our hearts desires are placed in us for a purpose; they are part of who we are, who we will become and whom we will serve.

I can't think of a more important vocation than to help others find success by learning to project a positive, confident image. This process can take a moment or a lifetime to learn and truly begins when we learn to Love, Live and Give passionately.

In closing, I leave an affirmation a parting gift: may it help you "Get Image Ready" for your purpose in life as you create fulfillment and happiness with your own version of beauty: "As my outward appearance and presentation aligns with my inner beauty and God-given purpose doors will open, deals will close and all the support I will ever need for success will find me."

Charlotte Howard

The Beauty Confidence Guru Charlotte Howard is a renowned Women Life Mentor, Award-Winning Hair Artist, Founder of Hair Artist Association, Founding Premier Member of Women Speakers Association, Success & Beauty Talk Radio Host, Publisher of Hair Artist Lifestyle Magazine, Creator of Heart Centered Women Publishing and 5x's Best Selling Author.

Charlotte's mission is to empower millions of women to discover fulfillment and happiness in their lives. She is all about women empowering women to create a renewed sense of energy and motivation for enhancing themselves, lives and business from the inside out!

Hire Charlotte for your next personal, business or life project. Get her FREE Audio Cd "Create a Beautiful, Confident New You Even During Tough Times" (a $97 value!)

Charlotte can be reached at:
Phone: (803) 414-2117 Skype: CharlotteEmryHoward
About Me | Brand Yourself | Hair Artist Association | Twitter | Facebook | Linkedin | Pinterest

CREATING A BEAUTIFUL, SEXY AND CONFIDENT NEW YOU BY CHARLOTTE HOWARD

Are you successful in some ways but underneath still feel that you could be stronger and feel more confident?

Most women I know are. If you are like most women you have had a traumatic experience or have been programmed from childhood on an ideal image of beauty, one few of us ever see reflected when we look in the mirror.

While growing up as a teenager I was raped, felt helpless and no longer felt beautiful from the inside out. I tried to take an overdose of pills as I was growing up hoping all the bad memories would go away. I finally told my mom ten years later because I was afraid of what others would think of me after being raped.

What held me together this hold time during my life journey? Having faith in god and having confidence in myself was the very first steps to moving forward with my journey in life.

After being raped I knew that I did not wish for any woman to ever get to a point in their life that they did not want to go on with their life because they felt helpless. It was that moment I pursued my journey to empower women to unlock their own beauty from the inside out.

I went to cosmetology school right after my high school completion and earned my degree in cosmetology. I began working in a corporate beauty salon for over a decade as an award-winning hair stylist/manager. I decided to walk away from corporate america to pursue my passion, purpose and dreams at deeper levels.

Are you struggling to create a beautiful, sexy and confident new you?

Here's how you can look in the mirror and despite the ideal, see only a beautiful you.

When you look in the mirror, what's the first thing you notice, and how does it make you feel?

If you're like most women, the first thing that catches your eye is probably your least favorite asset. If so, don't worry you're not alone. Here's why.

Can you guess how much money is spent in just one year by advertisers to sell us on the concept of the "ideal" image of beauty?

Well —it's billions of dollars!

So, technically, you can consider yourself brainwashed.

From your earliest childhood days—if you played with Barbie—you've been receiving constant, consistent images' telling you what beauty is supposed to look like.

Never mind that these images are for the most part, anatomically impossible!

And, would you really want to look like every celebrity you see?? Honestly?

I'm guessing probably not.

So, here's how you can build your confidence with the body God gave you:

1. Look in the mirror

2. This time, really look at yourself.

Reflect on the compliments you have received.

Do people tell you how great your hair is?

How beautiful your eyes are?

That you have a nice smile? Try to see what they see.

3. Stand far enough away from the mirror so that you can take it all in. What do you see? Find at least three positive things.

4. Now, get up close. Really close.

Look at your eyes—the irises. What color are they? Are they all one color or are there flecks of various colors? How would you describe them using positive analogies or adjectives?

5. Now, smile. What does your smile convey? Warmth? Happiness?

6. Find at least three characteristics you like best about yourself, and then accentuate them as you dress to go out.

- If you love your eyes, make sure your hair doesn't cover them up
- Love your lips? Make sure to keep them soft and moisturized
- Your hair? Get a flattering haircut and condition it regularly to keep it shiny and healthy. Change your hair color to bring out your beautiful skin tones

In short, amplify what you like, and don't worry about the parts you don't.

Here are some ways to do just that:

- Go shopping and bring a good friend. Ask them to help you pick out colors and clothes they think flatter you. Don't worry if your first reaction is "that's not me!" Experiment!
- Contact your image consultant and hair stylist to have them help you create a unique look and style that enhances you from the inside out.
- Feel better about whatever it is you don't like about yourself by picturing the absolute worst-case scenario. Exaggerate whatever it is you're hung up on and blow it up in your mind until it's comical. Then look in the mirror—not so bad anymore is it?
- Accept yourself for who you are, how you look, and focus on what really matters—the things about you that can't be seen —your heart, your mind and your soul!
- What do you want people to praise you for? Is it really how you look? Probably not. You probably want people to think you're funny, smart, nice, or generous—something along those lines right?
- Make a list of your positive personal qualities and characteristics. Then ask yourself, what's more important? Get involved in activities that build on your personal characteristics—volunteer, join a club, and take a class to sharpen your talents. These will help you emphasize and focus more on the more important qualities that get you through life successfully and with more fun.

Over the years, I've met a lot of successful women. A few were happy, a few not so much. Too many women swallowed the idea that "unhappiness" was called for "dues" along the path to success. Someday, once successful, they'll as if by magic get "happy." So many women are working day-and-night, missing family events, deserting passions, putting dreams on hold and missing out on their own happiness.

Simply put working themselves to death. However what if women might work themselves to life? What does Abundance and being happy imply to you? We all have our unique views and definitions of what abundance and being happy is. Abundance, being happy, harmony and fulfillment in life is decided and first produced on the inside. It all starts at the level of consciousness. Your consciousness.

By formulating an exquisite understanding that regardless of what you may currently be going through can be changed; by arriving at a conscious choice to be aware of and elevate the inner processes that are literally drawing in to you whatever those situations may be, you'll be well on the way to producing the abundance and being happy that you want to experience. You've been furnished the free will as well as the power to consciously produce your wanted results.

Formulate the awareness of how to switch the inner processes that are producing your present external results, and you'll have discovered the key to consciously producing whatever results that you really want in and for your life. Formulate the discipline to consistently apply your newfound cognizance, make the necessary "internal shift" that's harmonious with your "wanted" results and your life will reflect one of joyfulness, fulfillment, purpose, fundamental peacefulness and boundless successfulness.

Abundance and being happy really is readily available and really simply attainable when you understand how to align and harmonize with it in a conscious and intentional way. That's when you start to enable and allow yourself to draw in and experience the physical, financial, relational, mental, emotional and spiritual harmony we all want.

Live life, love fully and laugh often!

With Love,

Charlotte

Dr. Christina Kovalik

Dr. Christina Kovalik NMD, LAC, is a Naturopathic Medical Doctor and Acupuncturist. "Transforming Families Naturally". She is a family practitioner with a special interest in women's health specifically infertility, PMS, menstrual irregularities, hormone imbalances, fatigue, menopause, pre and post natal support, and Gynecology. Dr. Kovalik graduated from Southwest College of Naturopathic Medicine in Tempe, AZ, and the Phoenix Institute of Herbal Medicine and Acupuncture in Phoenix, AZ. She empowers her patients by treating the root cause of imbalance and thru education creating a ripple effect in all that they do.

http://drchristinakovalik.com

MY JOURNEY TO SUCCESS AND EMPOWERMENT
BY DR. CHRISTINA KOVALIK NMD, LAC. ·

My journey as a physician and interest in natural medicine started at a very early age. My mother used to teach childbirth education classes in our living room. I remember seeing pregnant moms learning about the birthing process. When I was 4, my mother brought me to a live birth of one of her clients. That experience set the stage for my interest in women's health, pregnancy and post partum health.

My father and step mother lived a very healthy lifestyle and expressed the importance of living that way by eating well, exercising, spending quality time with each other and having a balanced social life. My Dad has spinal stenosis affecting his neck and lumbar spine. He sought out traditional medical doctors who, at the time, stated that surgery would be his best option. Disgusted with that, he sought out natural alternatives. He utilized mineral therapies, chiropractic and core exercises to heal himself. This healthy lifestyle was ingrained in who I am and what I believe in.

When I was in college and medical school, I developed a strong interest in spiritual development and meditation by studying Buddhism and spiritualism. My intent was to develop my own intuition knowing that it would be a big part of how I practice today. I continue to develop my intuitive abilities. It is all about the spiritual journey and opening up my patients, friends and family to the possibilities.

After completing my bachelor's degree in Microbiology with a minor in Art history in 1999, I was compelled to continue my education and felt drawn to become an Acupuncturist. I had never had acupuncture done before but felt in my heart that I needed to learn it. Upon researching graduate schools, I stumbled on the Naturopathic school Southwest College of Naturopathic Medicine in Tempe AZ.

I had never heard about naturopathic medicine but found the principles resonated with me. I was excited to have the opportunity to be outside of the box of traditional medicine. I applied and was accepted. After starting the program, I applied to the Phoenix Institute of Herbal Medicine and Acupuncture to obtain a Masters in Acupuncture. The study of Acupuncture and the art came to me very easily. It was a nice balance with the heavy science load of the naturopathic school. I graduated in 2003 with both a Masters in Acupuncture and a Doctorate in Natural Medicine. I remember the strong sense of accomplishment at the Senior walk celebration. It was one of the most exciting moments in my life!

My intuitive abilities continue to grow and develop with studying Peruvian shamanism, the Quantumpathic Energy method and attending meditation retreats. It is a huge part of the mind, body, spiritual connection for myself and my ability to share it with my patients.

After graduate school, I started my family with my husband. The birth of our first son was a trying time. He had seizures shortly after birth and was in the NICU for 3 weeks over the Christmas holiday. That was the hardest time in my life, being separated from my son and not in control of when he would be able to come home. The same day he was able to come home, I was admitted in the hospital for a post partum hemorrhage.

That experience made me a stronger person and am eternally grateful for the fact that our son never had seizures since and he is a healthy beautiful boy. I ended up staying home with him for the first year of his life and felt blessed to be a part of that time. However, I felt mentally frustrated. I desired to get out and start my practice and use the skills I acquired.

Five months after having my first son, my health was taxed. I was diagnosed with hyperthyroidism. Thyroid imbalances often show up after a stressful event like childbirth. I went the traditional route to have it investigated and felt frustrated with how allopathic medicine is so fear based. I decided to utilize what I am passionate about, natural medicine. I used herbs, acupuncture, and energy work to address the emotional cause of my thyroid imbalance. I lowered my thyroid hormone and am working on shrinking the nodule on my thyroid. That experience showed me what it was like to be the allopathic patient and the power of natural medicine.

Energetically, it stemmed from the throat chakra (energy center in the throat area) symbolizing not speaking my truth. I studied Quantumpathic energy method with Sherry Anshara to address my thyroid. It changed my life, my family's lives and my patients by teaching me to break through outdated belief systems, traumas, and emotions that didn't serve me. By releasing them, I am able to consciously create the life that I desire. I continue to utilize these skills with my acupuncture treatments today by assisting patients in identifying what emotions, beliefs or limiting thoughts are hindering their healing.

After the birth of my second son, I decided to start my own practice as a Naturopathic Medical Doctor and Acupuncturist in 2007. Embarking on this new journey, I didn't have much business confidence. In many ways I saw myself as a timid little girl who was rather introverted and frightened of failure. My fears were holding me back from being successful in my business. Little did I know just how capable I was of making positive life changing decisions.

Another key element in my progression as a physician occurred when I broke out of my comfort zone and started doing some personal development work with Michael Bernoff. It forever changed my thinking and mindset towards progress and success. I started working on my internal communication, how I express myself to others and building confidence in myself and my abilities. In shifting my perspective, I was able to see my business grow and be a better communicator.

One of the trainings, focused on taking that leap of faith towards your dreams and not letting fear get in the way. At that time I was renting a small room in a chiropractor's office. I then, made the decision to move into my own office space. It was a dream of mine to have my own practice. The advice I received from the trainings was given to me at a time when I was spreading myself thin between two businesses and I believe it gave me the confidence to solely focus on my own practice. From that point on my practice had doubled in patient quality and profits. I was able to arrange a work schedule that comfortably fit around my family and lifestyle. I was grateful for the opportunity to push myself to grow, make progress and assist patients on their healing journey.

I am now the best me, I can be. I am more confident in what I have to offer my patients on their journey towards optimal health. I allow my true self to radiate through me confidently. I focus on creating a ripple effect on all I come in contact with by teaching others how to make healthy life changes to optimize their health and wellness. I am living my purpose to make a difference in the world while sharing my talents and gifts along the way.

How I have influenced my patients. The patients that I have helped over the years bring great joy in my heart. Especially when the patient follows my recommendations and they get better. My goal as a physician is to meet the patient where they are at and assist them in reaching their health goals naturally. I am passionate about assisting families naturally and especially love fertility, pregnancy, and post partum cases. I treated many patients successfully and honored them on their fertility journey. Each fertility patient has had different obstacles to overcome with a common goal, to create a sacred space for a baby and creating or expanding the family.

Kay* 37 year old female struggling with fertility challenges for her first child. Her husband's sperm is normal. She is fatigued and has irregular cycles with PMS symptoms. We spent 6 months preparing her body for pregnancy by treating her adrenal glands, regulating her menstrual cycle, treating her low progesterone and weekly acupuncture.

She realized that she didn't want to be like her mother, and had a fear associated with it. Once she realized it and released the fear, she became energetically clear and conceived a beautiful little girl.

Jackie* 28 year old female with absent menstrual period for 6 months. We tested her thyroid and progesterone which were low. We started weekly acupuncture, nutritional supplements and herbs and she became pregnant after 2 months even though she never had a period.

Susie* 34 year old- 35 weeks pregnant with her first child came to me for anxiety and a breech baby. She felt overwhelmed with the fact that she was working full time and didn't understand why her baby wouldn't turn. It turns out that the she never really connected to the baby inside her.

During an acupuncture session, we did a visualization to help her connect to the baby and had a conversation. She discovered that her own stresses and worries have influenced the baby. She started connecting to the baby daily and singing to it. The baby turned 2 weeks later and she delivered a healthy baby girl.

Tyler* 16 year old football player presented with Valley fever and was fatigued. He was currently on antifungal medication but it didn't seem to help with the fatigue. He stopped the antifungal medication, did a series of acupuncture treatments and herbal therapy and 2 months later there was no sign of valley fever. He continues to play football without any symptoms.

Empower yourself to make lasting changes to optimize your health and enjoy life's challenges and joys. By following my passion and helping others leaves a lasting impression. The body has innate powers to heal itself naturally given the correct environment (nutrients, releasing energetic/ emotional blockages, etc.). I empower my patients by teaching them to take control and optimize their health and wellness.

Darlene Alexander

Darlene Alexander is a licensed cosmetologist, trichologist, author and speaker. Darlene is the Vice President and Co-founder of Heavenly Essence, Inc., the creators of Pure'ity Hypo-allergenic hair care products. Her company partners with salons to provide their client's with quality products, hair loss solutions and education to enhance their services. Darlene also works with women and children to provide customized wigs.

Website: http://www.heavenlyessence.net
Blog: http://www.heavenlyessence.net/#!blog/c3om
Facebook: https://www.facebook.com/pureityhaircareproducts
Twitter: https://twitter.com/HeavenlyEssence
LinkedIn: http://www.linkedin.com/in/darlenealexander
Google Plus: https://plus.google.com/+HeavenlyessenceNet
Pinterest: http://www.pinterest.com/heavenlyessence
Instagram: @HeavenlyEssence
Email: pureity@heavenlyessence.net

FAITH THAT MOVES FEAR
BY DARLENE ALEXANDER

When I was a child, I was fortunate to have a strong support system. I was a strong-willed child, adventurous, but shy. I would play baseball in dresses, sliding into bases and skinning my knees. Yes I still have the scars to prove it. I remember riding a 10-speed bicycle to impress a boy I liked and I did not have knowledge about the bike or its brake system. Needless to say, I applied the brake hard, flipped off the bike, and landed in several bushes. Since I landed in bushes with thorns, I had some pricks from the thorns.

My last adventurous experience while wearing a dress was when my stepfather took me to the park to play. One day while at the park, I decided to climb a wire fence and I managed to tear my underpants. I was so embarrassed. However the worst part was not over, I had to approach my stepfather and tell him to take me home because I tore my underpants. The expression on his face was memorable. After arriving home, my mom was surprised to see us so soon. When she asked, my stepfather immediately told my mom, "Your daughter torn her underpants climbing a wire fence."

On a less adventurous day I would love to role play. One of my favorite roles was being a business owner. I had an area in our garage that I set up as my office. I used a table as my desk and confiscated an old telephone from my parents. I would talk on the phone, type letters and give orders to the younger kids. The second thing I loved to do was play with my Barbie mannequin head. This head had hair you could pull out through an opening at the top. I would cut and style, pull more hair out of the opening, cut and style it too. Eventually there was no more hair I could cut or style. By the time I realized her hair wasn't growing back, it was too late.

When I was a child, the fear of challenges were not an issue. I boldly was able to face and overcome them. It was not until I entered my early teens that I felt the crippling effects of fear. I participated in track in elementary school, but when I entered seventh grade it became less enjoyable because I felt I wasn't fast enough. In that same school year I experienced hair breakage, so then because I lost a portion of my hair I wasn't pretty enough. I kid you not, I wore a scarf the majority of seventh grade.

Then I tried to be creative with the scarf and wrap it around this 2-inch ponytail that I wore at the top of my head. I would bobby pin the scarf to my remaining hair so it would stay in place. Silly me I actually believed those bobby pins would hold the scarf in place. However, those bobby pins were no match when a person felt they just had to snatch the scarf off of my head. Imagine this, me running down the hall chasing a boy trying to retrieve my scarf so I could wrap it around my 2-inch ponytail and make it to my next class before the bell rang. I was thrilled when my hair started to grow back and by the beginning of eighth grade I had a new hairstyle.

As I entered high school, I struggled in my school work. I guess you can say I had struggled all along in school, but it became apparent in the tenth grade. Then came HOPE! The Word of God states in Jeremiah 29:11, For I know the plans I have towards you plans to prosper you and not to harm you to give you a hope and a future. My hope came through the Regional Occupational Program offered through the high school. I was given the opportunity to attend cosmetology school free of charge while   attending high school.

This opportunity allowed me to dream again. A spirit of creativity was birthed. A new challenge to overcome. A door of opportunity was opened to be who God created me to be – it all came alive in me. Wow!!!!
However as I moved closer to graduating from cosmetology school, once again fear came rearing its evil head. Who do you think you are? You will never pass that examination. You are too afraid to travel to even take the exam.

Yes fear (False Evidence Appearing Real) almost stopped me in my tracks, but God had a plan. My mom, Margree Handley Gafford, had brought up the fact that I successfully completed 1600 hours of cosmetology school and now I'm telling her I'm not taking the examination. She told me, "You are taking that examination." After convincing me to take the examination, my mom spoke to the lady I had asked to be my model. She asked her to drive my car to San Francisco, so I could take my state board examination.

My mom knew I wasn't ready to tackle the bay area traffic, but she knew I was capable of passing that examination. That mountain (the bay bridge) was standing in my way; without my mother's help I would have allowed that bridge to keep me from my destiny. Let me explain my fear. I had been driving for only a couple of months and it decided to snow. I pleaded and begged my parents to take me to school, but they told me I need to learn how to drive in the snow.

Their only instruction was do not wait until the last minute to brake or you'll slide. They failed to advise me about hills. As I was entering the school's parking lot, I had to climb a hill. Now as I was climbing the hill, I was sliding backwards and my classmates were watching me and laughing. Eventually I gave up, turned the car around, and went into another parking lot – one without a hill. Hopefully my snow experience has shed some light on why I didn't want to travel across a bridge surrounded by water as far as the eye could see. I wasn't ready to endure that feat.

I'm sure you probably guessed we made it safely across the bay bridge into San Francisco. The bridge didn't collapse, the water stayed in its place, and my fears of failing the examination were unfounded. I passed with flying colors. After receiving my cosmetology license I worked as a stylist, but eventually I went back to school to further my education. Over the years I worked in several industries, a non-profit recreational center, legal, law enforcement and the medical field. All while maintaining my cosmetology license and staying connected with the latest trends in the beauty industry.

A desire rose inside of me to return to the beauty industry with a purpose – this time to make a difference. Again, God had a plan. A mountain I encountered (sickness), lead me back to my first love. After taking several years off to regroup and heal, it was time to spread my wings and fly. In 2005, my family and I formed our company Heavenly Essence, Inc., and in 2008 Pure'ity Hypoallergenic hair care products was birthed. Our products were developed because of my sensitivities to synthetic ingredients in hair care products. My hope is with our products we can help others with similar product sensitivities find a solution to their problem.

Our products are now in salons, health and wellness stores, and beauty supply stores. We have expanded our operations to help women and children with hair loss. We specialize in custom-made wigs and hair loss solutions.

Remember I said earlier as a child I was shy. I'm still shy. God clearly has a sense of humor. He has placed me, Darlene Alexander in public speaking roles. Picture this, as I'm speaking at beauty schools my son, Sheldon is in the background telling me to speak up because I'm speaking too softly. Wow!!! Another mountain that has to move out of my way.

As I reflect upon my childhood, having an office set up in my families' garage with a table as a desk, typewriter, telephone, bossing the younger kids around, cutting and styling my Barbie mannequin until there was no more hair to cut or style. Now I know I was destined to be a business owner and cosmetologist and fear nearly hindered my dream.

Have you stopped dreaming? Don't give up on your dreams. Ignite your faith and do not allow fear or circumstances to hinder your success. One of my favorite scriptures is Hebrews 11:1 NOW faith is the substance of things hoped for the evidence of things not seen. You can't see the outcome, but you have faith it will manifest and work in your favor. I'm convinced that what I did, you can do and you can do it better. You have it in you…Faith that moves fear!

Diane Aiello

Diane Aiello has spent over twenty seven years as a makeup artist in the fashion and commercial industry working with clients such as Vanity Fair, Allure, Michael Kors, Antonio Banderas and Glenn Close. She lives out her purpose of creating confidence and uplifting others not only as a working makeup artist and fashion stylist but as a coach and mentor helping other artists to gain clarity, push past barriers and reach their goals to sustain a successful career and live a life they love. She is also the owner of Glam Lounge Artists on-location makeup and hair team.

www.mybeautymuse.com
www.glamlounge.net

BEYOND ADVERSITY BY DIANE AIELLO

As we closed the car door and drove away we both noticed something sounded really funny. The cool night air swooshed through the back of the rental car making unfamiliar rattling sounds. The Art Director said, "Oh my gosh Diane we've been robbed." In disbelief I turned to look back to where my hair and makeup kits, wardrobe kits and wardrobe had been, only to see chips of glass scattered everywhere. My heart sunk. It was at the end of the first day of a two-day photo shoot. We had stopped for a crew dinner after wrapping that night. Sadly, I broke my own rule, at the urging of others and against my better judgment, which I vocalized—I left the kits and wardrobe in the car and now it was all gone.

The client would have to pay for the borrowed wardrobe totaling over $20,000, and I estimated my own personal loss was over $9,000. I was devastated, overcome by guilt, fear, and anger; you name it, I was feeling it. Back at the hotel after the police reports and phone call to my husband it hit me: I needed to figure out the second day of shooting. Thankfully, I put the day's wardrobe in my assistant's car, but I still had to do hair and makeup. With the handful of products that were in my toiletry bag and the model's own makeup we made it happen and the photos were gorgeous. Relief!

Through it all I was trying to maintain faith and trust that God had a plan, a plan that was bigger than I could understand. I believe that faith and trust is a practice—it doesn't just happen one day when you have a crisis. God had been working in me by growing my faith and trust significantly over the last few years. I always trusted him with my freelance business, even when I struggled as a new makeup artist often selling my clothes to resale stores or eating ramen for days to pay the bills. When I wasn't bold, he was bold for me. I trusted when my beauty boutique and spa went from fledgling to successful to failing.

I exercised my trust muscle through practice, much like a yoga practice or a workout in the gym to build muscle and lose fat. I trusted when we lost everything and filed bankruptcy. I trusted when I rebuilt my business. I needed to trust again, with just twenty-four hours before I was flying to New York for Fashion Week to work. I was booked on seven shows, five of them with one of the artists I looked up to the most. I had set a goal of being on her team two years earlier and I refused to show up unprepared.

I had one day to prep, pack and get a grip on my emotional state. The theft came just days after my beloved pet Coco of twenty years, my baby when I didn't have babies, had to be put to sleep. Amidst the loss and the tears and emotions, my mantra became "be strong, be faithful and trust."

Most people think the life of a makeup artist is glamorous and "fun." When I coach and mentor other makeup artists, I often have to cut through misconceptions. I'm not going to lie, it is fun, but it's also a job and a journey that requires grind, determination, sacrifice and perseverance. When I am on set working with multi-million dollar companies on their ad campaigns, fashion magazines or catalog shoots, I have a responsibility. To serve, support, and deliver the look that the client needs for their end result.

In the last few hours before heading to the airport for New York Fashion Week, I received an email cancelling me from not one, not two, not three, but all 5 shows working alongside the artist I had dreamed of working with.

I arrived in New York still feeling crushed from the past week's events. As I finished the first of only two remaining bookings that week, I received an email to help on a shoot for Vogue Magazine happening within the hour ...YES, yes, yes I can do it! Minutes later I was practically skipping down Ninth Avenue with makeup kits in tow when sadly I received a call saying they no longer needed me.

Amidst all the craziness to re-center myself each day I got quiet, I prayed and meditated. I tried to trust but I know I wasn't giving it my all. That week I sat having coffee with a few fellow artists, all younger with shorter resume's but no less drive or passion, as they were getting last minute calls for more and more shows. No matter how hard it was for me, I was happy to see these eager artists getting such great gigs—I certainly didn't want to detract from their accomplishments. I am rooted in the belief that we each have a purpose and path that is uniquely ours and only mine is mine.

Ask any accomplished person and they will tell you failure is often the precursor to success. Coming up in the business I expected that failure might be a part of the process, but now our society treats failure as the new version of the "f" word. Other artists look at my career and resume' and assume I have it easy. Perhaps in some ways I do, but what they don't see is the messiness along the way, the obstacles, the sacrifices and times of doubt and adversity. Joanna Schlip a respected makeup artist was asked "I've been working hard for months, how long do I have to struggle?" She responded, " Honey, the hustle never ends…" Our expectations for success are set so high and we want it quickly, but when it doesn't happen as we imagined it creates frustration, depression and defeat. But when you are cloaked in defeat, you can't be in a position to receive. When you have one foot dragging in shame, defeat or old baggage you build a barrier between you and your purpose. Life and careers ebb and flow. Some seasons we are cutting back the unneeded branches and planting new seeds and in the right season we reap the harvest.

In my life, during times of adversity I have been fortunate to have an amazing supportive husband, family and friends who believed in me even when I didn't, who lifted me when I couldn't. A positive support system is priceless… don't expect them to be perfect but find those people who will be your strength when you are weak.

So, I wasn't meant to work for Vogue… This time… I wasn't meant to work with one of my idols in the industry for five shows… This time. Maybe it was time to let go of my makeup kit and get outside of my comfort zone so that I could step up my artistry skills.

I know with certainty that every adversity shapes you for a future that you don't even know about yet and, every hardship helps to build the bridge that takes you from the dreams you conceive to the dreams you receive. The good part is it's not your place to always understand why. On a spiritual level, I trust God and stay faithful and open to his purpose for me while taking one step at a time.

When you have a goal, or a dream for your future, your life, your career, your family your road will be littered at times with obstacles, and when you find them go through them, around them, or over them whatever it takes to get beyond them. It's not how many times you are knocked down but how many times you get back up.

Those two weeks in 2013 pushed me forward and motivated me in a way I could not have imagined. Six months later I returned to New York Fashion Week and had the honor of working with someone who has inspired me for over twenty years. Subsequently I have worked with magazines in the Vogue family of publications, my on-location makeup team has nearly doubled in size and my coaching business for makeup artists has not only grown but fostered a positive community of artists uplifting each other on their journey. Plus, I've created an online course to help emerging artists achieve a full time freelance career. The adversity I faced helped me to step further into my purpose and serve others in a bigger way.

Today, wherever you are, whatever is challenging you, look inside and find your purpose.

To stay inspired make a list of the top things that motivate you to achieve your dreams and read them every day. Center yourself in faith and believe in someone bigger than you. Know that there is a master plan and the path meant for others is not the same unique plan meant for you.

Elinor Stutz

Elinor Stutz, CEO of Smooth Sale, is an inspirational speaker. Stutz' incredible journey begins with a surgeon's prediction of paralysis due to a broken neck, to fighting for her life using belief, vision and sales skills. Four days later she walked out of the hospital with a new vision of empowering others. Audiences are brought to their feet providing standing ovations.

Let's Connect:
Twitter: @smoothsale
Youtube: Elinor Stutz
LinkedIn: Elinor Stutz

Smooth Sale
www.smoothsale.net
408-209-0550
elinor@smoothsale.net

UNLOCKING MY SMOOTH SALE
BY ELINOR STUTZ

My 55th birthday will always be the most memorable. Joy was mine sharing the day with my family. But that particular day turned into a very dark and rainy night. The roads were slick. Returning home, the car made a slow left turn. We experienced the car skidding slowly and deliberately into a light pole. Everyone was fine except for me. I heard myself saying in a soft voice, "I think you better call an ambulance."

The ambulance arrived swiftly. Taking one look at me in the back seat, the attendant gently instructed, "Mrs. Stutz, do not attempt to get out of the car. We will take every required precaution to help you." He and his attending help expertly removed me from the car and then placed me onto a makeshift bed inside the ambulance. The final touch was placement of a large neck brace.

I viewed the ride to Stanford Hospital as a new opportunity to finally get the desired required care. My mind drifted back to how this predicament developed. Ten years prior, I was stopped at a red light waiting for it to turn green. In a swift instant everything changed. A young mother, driving in the car behind me, was physically turned around talking to her little children in the backseat. Moving at full speed, the force of her car produced a tremendous collision into the rear of mine.

A doctor visit was required. I shared that upon impact I could actually feel my brain swaying inside my head. Over the years, occasional shooting pain was felt from my neck down through my spine, but I was told I had to learn to live with the pain.

As I rode in the ambulance due to the second accident, I felt relief and held hope that my neck would finally be repaired. The exact moment of when the X-ray results came back is where my unusual story begins.

My immediate family was standing in a small room with the surgeon on call only a few feet away. They saw that my spine was very close to resembling the letter Z. There was no way for it to be repaired. Suddenly, loud sobbing was heard as the surgeon tried in vain to prepare my family that my best possible outcome would be paralysis.

At that exact moment of hearing sobbing, my life flashed in front of me in the form of a report card. On the left-hand side, I had very high "life" marks. Quickly glancing over to the right-hand side of the report card, I became deeply embarrassed. The column header read, "Community Service".

There I lay with a blank page on my conscience. My time had literally come. It was in that very instant that I made a promise to myself and negotiated with the great beyond. I pledged, should I be able to walk out of the hospital, I would begin giving back to communities at large. The promise was delivered with every ounce of my being. Fortunately, my inner voice heard me. Next, a voice deep within asked, "Do you believe you will be well?"

I tried to take my mind off the sobbing in the background but it was difficult to ignore. Straddling belief and reality, I responded, "I think I'm going to be well."

The voice returned with a harsh reality saying, "No, Elinor, that's not good enough. I'll ask you again. Do you believe you are going to be well?"

Responding silently to the voice deep within, and with profound conviction, I said, "I want to be well and will do everything imaginable to make it happen."

The pledge was made with every ounce of energy remaining. Next, an even more startling second vision appeared. A vivid generic figure stood in front of me. The human resemblance appeared as if it were standing on a mound speaking to audiences far and wide. A gold light was reflected behind the figure and then slowly expanded to cover my entire body.

The figure represented me. As the sobbing in the background grew louder, doubt crept back. Concern was shared with my inner voice that the figure didn't look like a female. I was wondering if that figure truly represented me. The voice came back taking on a deep concerned tone asking, "Do you doubt that can be you?" Instantly, I recognized a need to rise in every sense to the occasion.

"No," I responded. "I don't doubt that can be me. I want to grow into becoming an international speaker. This would be my dream come true."

My inner voice then proclaimed, "This is your last opportunity. Do you believe you are going to be well and rise to become that speaker? Will you keep your promise to help communities worldwide?"

With a fervent "YES!" I silently declared I would do whatever was necessary to grow into becoming that person reflected before me and vowed there would be no stopping me. I took one last and serious look at the vision and light to watch it all fade away. The entire experience of the two visions only took about one minute, during which I had been completely sheltered from my family.

At the exact moment the visions disappeared, my family walked over to me with tears streaming down their faces. Given what just transpired, I tried to comfort and assure them I would recover. While my family was in despair, I was so excited about what happened on that stretcher. In my mind, I believed 100% that I would be well.

An almost meditative state of mind came over me examining my priorities for creating a business. At the top of my list were working with a high level of customer service and integrity. I believe, when you move with integrity there will never be a need to change your story. My first business plan was mentally prepared in ICU.

I was on a natural high, even when screws were literally hammered into my forehead to hold a metal halo in place. The stroke of luck came when a visiting brain surgeon stopped by to see how I was doing.

He explained weights are customarily attached to the halo to aid the straightening of the spine prior to surgery. The norm was to attach five pounds but, the norm wasn't working. He suggested an experiment of attaching sixty pounds of weight.

There was no hesitation on my part. The instant the extra weight was attached I felt immediate relief. As the brain surgeon relayed results of his experiment to his students of placing the extra weight to my spine, some gasped. Others looked as if their eyes would pop out of their head.

The next morning, excitement took hold given everything that transpired. I was taken to anesthesiology to be heavily medicated for surgery. I knew whole-heartedly that I would finally be well. The anesthesiologist forewarned I would only have 1.5 minutes to speak with the surgeon and then the administered medication would put me into a deep slumber.

To my horror, I heard the surgeon tell me in no uncertain terms, "Mrs. Stutz, when you wake up, you will most likely be paralyzed."

Business skills and the power of belief saved my life. Standing before me was a highly trained surgeon to whom I will be eternally grateful. If I had accepted his statement as fact, my life would have ended, as I knew it. The clock was ticking with the medication making its way into my system with only 30 seconds remaining.

My response was delivered by locking my eyes on his. Next, I copied the tone of his voice, look on his face, and used some of his vocabulary. I replied with all of the strength left within by saying, "Doctor, when I wake up, I fully expect to be well!"

I remember seeing the startled surgeon actually jump backwards. Hours later as I was awakening, the surgeon was standing over me. I heard him softly say,"Mrs. Stutz, There is no explanation for what took place, but in four days you will walk out of this hospital."

Much of the medical staff came to visit me to see the woman who believed so strongly she would be well that, she became well. The staff referred to me as a "walking miracle."

Four days later, I was released. I was on a quest to find the meaning of the gold light. Years later, I was introduced to an Asian alternative healthcare doctor. It was as if a thunderbolt of lightening hit as I heard her say, "After a severe accident the best chance for recovery is when a gold light appears over the entire body. We are magnetic fields of energy and the gold light represents our cells working at a rapid rate to accelerate healing. "

I accepted the story as true. The entire story is now shared with the purpose of encouraging many to help communities. Together we may positively impact society. Doing so ultimately leads to the Smooth Sale!

Fawn Cheng

Fawn Cheng is a nationally known Personal Stylist and Image consultant. She is regularly featured in the media for fashion and lifestyle tips and privately consults with clients to transform their wardrobe, image, and personal confidence in a way that gives them a competitive edge. Cheng's instincts and refined eye enables her unique insight to identify each person's unique X Factor; this is then woven into their personal style.

The result?
A look that is fresh, hip, and unabashedly Bombshell.

Fawn meets objectives with finesse, sensitivity, and creativity; this has earned her praise in the fashion and styling industry. Visit www.fawncheng.com

DROP IT LIKE A BOMBSHELL BY FAWN CHENG

The bombshell. We all know one.

She's bold, bodacious, and unapologetic about her beauty. The bombshell's confidence is one of her greatest features, but where does it come from? It comes from her quiet conviction that real beauty emanates from her radiant self-acceptance and her genuine care for others. While she knows that, yes, beauty has something to do with looking her best, it's more about the work she does on the inside. This matters first because this inside job grows that confidence and gives her the radiance that makes her irresistible.

The bombshell is free and as such, she's not afraid to take risks. She views her physical body as a blank canvas, meant to outwardly express her inner beauty. You can easily spot her because she celebrates femininity in the way she creates her image and flirts with her makeup, hair, and clothes. Every day gives her a chance to play dress-up; she loves being a woman and it shows! The bombshell knows she shines and rather than tip toe around her bright light, she scouts for, then acknowledges, light in others and engages the world in a way that people leave her presence feeling radiant too.

Want to be a bombshell? I passionately believe you have all the makings to be!

As a personal stylist I have a unique opportunity to help people realize their own bombshell-ness. For me, it isn't about putting clients in something simply because it's a name brand or the hottest trend. It also isn't about pumping empty compliments to give them a false sense of themselves. Whether they consciously recognize it or not, my clients are sharing an intimate vulnerability with me. It's not easy standing in front of an expert, allowing her to scan you head to toe and give you an honest appraisal of your current image.

It wouldn't be easy for me either, so I carefully accept and guard this vulnerability with non-judgment and fuse it with a heartfelt ambition to extract and communicate my client's radiance back to her. I have tall clients, short clients, skinny and oversize ones, and in more than seven years of styling, I've yet to work with a client that I didn't find brilliant when we completed our session. Why? Is it because I only work with the "beautiful people"? Well actually, yes! A beloved mentor once told me to stay unfailingly present and intentional in all of my pursuits. And this advice works!

The primary objective is the blaring intention to look deeper and scout the essence of another person's beauty. I always find it, because it's not hard to do, and this filters my interactions with them. I don't have to sugar coat feedback because with an intention for finding beauty, unconditional acceptance, and a healthy dose of non-judgment, people are open to receiving critical feedback. What's better is that they are also open to receiving praise...and this is where magic happens! I revel in the moments when a client's assurance and self-acceptance begins to show.

So that was a primer on how to mirror another's bombshell nature. But how often do you do this for yourself? Remember earlier when I mentioned "real beauty emanates from her radiant self-acceptance"? The bombshell knows her greatest gift is to shine so she can emanate light for others, but she's got to shine in her own eyes too!

Do you ever stop to listen to your thoughts about yourself? We get so busy in the hustle and bustle, we rarely stop to pay attention to the things we tell ourselves. If you stopped right now and listened to your internal dialog, what would you hear?

If you aren't inundating yourself with a long to-do list, you've probably got an endless stream of random, truncated useless thoughts, images, and emotions, peppered with some heavy self-critiquing and unhealthy comparisons to others. Pick up the mail, drop off the laundry, pay the bills, work faster, eat less, exercise more.

When you do stop to become aware of your mindless chatter, it turns to; "This is a waste of time...I have so much to do...my belly is bloated...I should go for a run...I better skip lunch today...my thighs aren't responding to the treadmill anymore. Oh no, I'm getting fat!" We let this incessant stream of expectation and draining emotions drive the minutes of our days.

Have you ever asked yourself if this does you any good? If you could choose your self-talk, self-pictures, and self-emotions, what would you choose?

The bombshell knows how to drop useless, droning negativity and choose the thoughts, pictures, and emotions that move in her mind. She knows this is where her point of power exists and she doesn't compromise that mental space with anything that doesn't propel her in a positive and uplifting direction.

An experiment by Harvard social psychologist, Ellen Langer, in 1979 and replicated independently in 2010 showed that how you conceive of yourself and the environment created to support it, can have a profound effect on objective reality. A group of 75 year-old men were taken into retreat and lived in an environment and performed as if they were decades younger during that time. Prior to their going into sequestration, they were given a battery of tests and performed specific tasks.

Additionally, a separate group of unbiased individuals was shown a picture of each 75 year-old man and was asked to guess his age. After the retreat, those men were given the same battery of tests and tasks, and a new group of individuals were shown their "After" pictures and asked to guess their age. The results? Each man performed better on the tests and the average age guessed from their pictures went down by three years!

What valuable information can you extract from these experiments? If you really want it, you too can conceive of yourself as a bombshell and evolve into this reality through conscious choices and behavior.

Here is a little help to get you started. First, make a list of the bombshell things you want for yourself. Don't short change anything; really think through this. What do you look like, your body, face, hair? How do you feel? What are you wearing and where are you? What's your mood? How are you shining your light and even more, how are you helping others shine theirs? Are you catching my drift, here?

Set aside 5 minutes each day to sit quietly. Bring your attention to your breath. You will soon notice its rhythm slow down; your inhales will be slightly longer than your exhales. Now bring your attention to the stream of chatter that's running through your mind. It is much like that ticker tape that runs at the bottom of the TV screen on the news channels. The headlines shout all kinds of messages.

Simply observe them. Let all the headlines and pictures float across your mind. Don't latch on to any of them; the ones you like or the ones you dislike. Just notice they are there. If you inadvertently hook onto one, just let it go.

Creating this mental space gives you tiny distance from the non-stop ticker tape of self-talk and fragmented messages that subconsciously filter your perception of the world. Your starting point is to close your eyes and simply notice your breath. Feels good, doesn't it?

This exercise also offers you a nice little reprieve anytime you need peace of mind. Once you've gotten some practice at separating yourself from what Buddhist call this 'monkey mind', you are prepared to start an intention-based meditation. You have a choice in what's sailing across that noggin of yours.

Review the bombshell list you made earlier. Take about 5 or 10 minutes to sit quietly. Close your eyes and begin again noticing your breath. Let your thoughts roll in and out, not latching onto any. Now, reflect back on that bombshell list. Breathe every item in and out. The feelings, what you're doing, what you look like, how you show up for others. Wash yourself in this vision with every inhale and propel it into the world on your exhale. Head to toe and all over again. Don't break away from it. Feel it as if it's right here, right now.

With daily repetition, you'll soon notice subtle changes your life. This is the essence of dropping the negative self-talk and consciously replacing it with your highest vision for yourself. This is where the bombshell soars; she's a master in the art of dropping the negativity and now you know how to drop it like a bombshell too.

Go on, be a bombshell. I'm cheering you on!

Dr. Karen Jacobson

Dr. Karen Jacobson, affectionately known as "Dr. J" has been serving the community since 1992, sharing a message of Health and Healing through a variety of print, radio and television media including 12 News Long Island, 12News WKPNX, Cox 7-AZ, KAZTV and Design & Lifestyle Channel. She was the official Wellness Advisor Healthy U TV Show. She is honored to share her stories with the world as a multi-published author in three books: "Change Your World" "Chicken Soup for the Soul: Miracles Happen" and International bestseller "Ready, Aim, Inspire!"

As a High Performance Strategist she focuses on the Mind-Body Connection which elevates your health, career and human potential. She coaches CEO's, entrepreneurs, athletes and individuals who choose to operate at a high performance in life with the desire to improve their mind, body and spirit, to create overall wellness. By blending Intuition with Science, Dr. Jacobson provides you the Keys to Unlock Your Ultimate Potential and Live an Extraordinary Life! Take the first step to unlock your future - Claim your Free E-book at www.drkarenjacobson.com For booking and programs email drj@drkarenjacobson.com or call 480.447.MIND

LET YOUR INNER LIGHT SHINE THRU
BY DR. KAREN JACOBSON

She handed me her lip gloss and phone as she was about to go on stage. I watched her step into her glory, letting her inner light shine through. Her performance brought the room to their feet. I was so proud to see how my client embraced herself fully, sharing herself authentically with the audience.

Can you remember how you felt the last time you had to speak your mind in front of people? Whether in a group or one-on-one? Were you totally free or were you worried what people might think? I remember myself as a little girl, there were so many things that I had wanted to say or wanted to do but didn't. I was always concerned about fitting in.

I was six years old when my family had picked up and moved overseas. I remember being excited for the new adventure in my life, especially the flight on a big 747 jumbo jet airplane. Things were quite different when we got to our destination. We moved to Israel, new country, new customs and new language. Everything was foreign and so was I. Even though I was in kindergarten, I don't really remember much of that time because of the language barrier.

By the time I started first grade I had met a few other kids from the US and we all took Hebrew language class together. Shortly thereafter we had become proficient in Hebrew and seemed to have blended in with the rest of the class. A couple of months into the school year I was picked as a child protégé to help a math professor create a new curriculum for elementary school, once again I felt singled out.

In fourth grade I was sent to an experimental class for gifted children. There were about 40 of us from all over the city got picked up by taxicabs every morning, were taught Russian and binary math as well as other advance studies.

The atmosphere in the class was highly competitive, a group of highly intelligent 10-year-olds who would do anything to be noticed and get a better grade but had no social skills or friendships. I was miserable, I worked really hard yet had no one to play with or connect with. After one semester I begged my mother to let me go back to my regular elementary school.

By then the damage was done. Little 10-year-old kids can be really mean. I was picked on and called names because I was different, I was the "smart kid". All I wanted was to have friends and belong. You can probably relate to that; whether your own experience or maybe even your children, one of our basic human needs is love and connection. That's why people live in communities, families or tribes.

Quite frankly, the older I got the worse things got. My desire to belong and be the same as others had caused me to start hiding parts of myself. It also didn't help that I had received advice from grown-ups telling me that I was "too much" for people to handle, too smart, too intense, too witty. I was told that maybe if I "dial it down" when meeting people and appear less than who I really was, I might make more friends.

Looking back I think to myself, that was interesting advice. Would you tell your son or daughter to pretend they are less smart than whom they really are just to be liked and make friends? By the time I was in eighth grade things had come to a head. I experienced public ridicule and bullying and wanted to change schools. As soon as I finished the last year of middle school I moved to a private high school.

Sadly things didn't change by changing high schools. Most of the students at the new school had been together since first grade; I was the new girl, the outsider and had a rough time yet again. Needless to say I was miserable. I was no longer the joyful, positive, inquisitive child I used to be. I was sad, negative and depressed.

By my junior year I got sick. I developed a butterfly shaped rash on my face that looked like a third degree burn. I had spent the following four years in and out of hospitals. Definitely not what your average teenager expects to do. Most teenagers expect to enjoy their last two years in high school and then go off to a good college, play sports or get a scholarship. Back then in Israel teenagers were expected to enlist in the Army and serve their country. My dream was to be an officer and commander.

Though I was sick, I still got to serve in the Army, but didn't have my dream job. Having been diagnosed with systemic lupus prevented me from strenuous physical activity or sun exposure. My only options were positions that confined me to the indoors and a desk. Until one day things came to a head. I have had enough; I chose to stand up to my commanding officer who was a vicious, abusive bully and refused an order. I didn't care that she was yelling at me from the top of her lungs or that I would be court-martialed. I was done; I was willing to deal with the consequences.

Soon thereafter I was hospitalized again and when I got out of the hospital, I spent two months in a military "spa like" facility that provided R&R to the wounded and sick soldiers. I remember my roommate telling me when I first got home, that the light had come back to my eyes. I was transferred out my old unit and spent the last six months of my service as a noncommissioned officer, second-best to my dream job. A week after I got out of the Army I was back in the states.

Moving back to the states accelerated my healing and allowed me to step back into my power. After tearing a hamstring I got to a chiropractor's office and ultimately healed myself naturally from lupus. My spiritual journey continued through doing a lot of inner work, Louise Hays book "you can heal your life" was pivotal in creating change for me. I chose to give back and help others and enrolled in chiropractic school. Not long after graduation I got to walk on fire with one of my mentors Tony Robbins, an experience that ignited my own inner fire.

While in private chiropractic practice I had the opportunity to see people from all walks of life. People who have come in with physical pain, yet the cause was emotional. People who woke up one day to realize the life they were living was not the life of their choice. That conflict lead to emotional stress causing a breakdown in their body. Watching people hold themselves back from living their ultimate potential is what drove me to becoming a high performance strategist, so I can help them break from decisions that were ultimately made long ago when they were children. Children are like sponges.

What you are told, you see as truth. Parents, teachers, preachers and the people around you will give you their opinion about anything you do and how you should live your life. Your subconscious mind embraces those beliefs as your own. Some may serve you and protect you when you're small, yet hold you back in adulthood. Think about it , have you ever found yourself in a situation, where you didn't want to say no to someone because they might get hurt? Have you ever done something because you were expected to? Maybe you're one of those who chose a career path that your parents wanted for you, even though your dreams were different; you never wanted to disappoint them. Maybe you grew up knowing you were different but wanted to belong, wanted to be part of the community rather than an outcast.

Maybe you grew up being told that children are best seen not heard and even though you're an adult, you still embrace that belief. It is time to break free and live your own life. Learn to embrace your uniqueness, to love what makes you different and allow yourself to fully express who you are, share your talents and your gifts with the world around you. For years I lived my life making other people happy. Doing what was expected of me, doing the right thing not necessarily what was right for me. That made me sick and miserable. I chose a different path. Rather than becoming less of who I am, I chose to be more of who I am. It is part of the journey.

I believe life is a gift, I believe you are a gift, inside of you there is a light, a potential that is unique only to you, it is time to unlock your ultimate potential, express, engage and experience your dream life!

Kellie R. Stone

In Kellie's quest to guide women on their journey of self-discovery, she is an avid student of life. This Life-Purpose Visionary, Inner Journey Strategist, and Intuitive Energy Healer received her coaching certification through renowned spiritual life and business coach, Karen Coffey and her attunement through Reiki Master, Christine McKenna-Eartheart. You'll discover Kellie's published articles on her women's global community, Womenslifelink.com and on Livestrong.com, Allthingschic.com, awakeningthegoddesswithin.net, Coffeytalk.com, Goddesslifestyleplan.com and many other blogs. Her published books include, The Butterfly Payoff: a woman's guide to defining purpose, fulfilling dreams, and getting paid for it and Are You Out of Your Freakin' Mind?.

ESCAPE FROM THE GUILLOTINE
BY KELLIE R. STONE

After the seventh stick to find a vein for an IV, my thoughts tumbled to a serene place miles in the past—before visits to the ER, debilitating head pain and nausea, and before my daily routine included ingesting five medications and fighting thoughts of decapitating myself. Yeah, that was me, sitting on the hospital gurney —a woman with chronic migraine disease, mounting despair, and crippling medical bills. It wasn't too long ago.

I really can't show you my enlightenment unless I first reveal the darkness of the dungeon in which I lived for the better part of 10 years during the prime of my life. I was just shy of my 35th birthday when I first noticed the frequency of headaches that had just come from time-to-time up to that point. You should also know that my health wasn't exactly a pristine blanket of white snow; it more resembled the yellow spotted area where your dog whizzes in the winter. Already sick with Fibromyalgia and Depression, I also contracted a wicked case of negative-thinking-osis.

I especially remember this time because it was around September 11, 2001. Granted, no one felt great in their minds, bodies or spirits during and after the tragedy of that day. My issues jack-hammered a little deeper. I was taken to the ER by my family after I emerged from the bathroom shaking, extremely nauseated, and quite unable to speak normally. "Kellie, did you just have a stroke?" "Are you dying?" "What the hell?" Scary questions bombarded my mind. You can imagine what my family asked, trying to make sense of my bizarre behavior.

That particular visit to the ER—the first of many—I will never forget. I was accused of overdosing on drugs by three different nurses, given an anti-psychotic medication, and sent on my way with no diagnosis.

Humiliation and fear dominated. It wasn't until I went to my family doctor that I learned it was a complex migraine, of which, at the time, not many doctors were familiar. You know those situations you wish were a dream, during which, if you only had a magic needle, you would just pop the bubble of reality and return to normal life?

Yeah, my life painted that abstract in the following days, months, and years when a couple of migraines became what seemed like one long one—enter stage left, the innretractable headache. Only, I didn't have a magic needle or even a clue how and why this horrible condition had chosen me. After all, I was a good person; I cared about my life and others; I just didn't deserve it! I was a victim of cruel circumstances. Or, so I thought. The guillotine taunted.

Fortunately, the complex migraine had not been a regular visitor to my world, at least until several years later. I was working on a Sunday afternoon when the migraine Grinch, once again, stole my proverbial Christmas. My concerned co-worker rushed me to the nearest ER, where, thankfully, they knew what was happening to me. After a few days and doses of Morphine, steroids and Phenergan, I came out of the disturbing episode that lynched my ability to speak or keep my head and hands from shaking. This began my journey with Neurologists and a season when my health adversely affected my family and professional life. My personal life was an arid wasteland, and I was fired from my job. "Just wonderful," I thought, "No job and more bills."

Bedridden and in a depressive funk, I curled up with my body pillow, wishing for a reason—a purpose for it all. I prayed. I begged. The result of my petitions was, however, the beginning of a new season for me. I returned to a former love abandoned in the cob-webbed hall of discarded dreams: Writing. Now, understand, my unplanned trip to the banks of becoming a writer wasn't dazzling, and it wasn't to help people or share my message of empowerment or hope. Instead, it was a greenie attempt to write a fiction crime novel. Regardless of my genre choice, writing became my outlet—a distraction from the pain and dysfunction crippling my life.

I could control my characters. My protagonist's migraine headaches had purpose, even if mine didn't. I'm a firm believer that it's never too late to be who you are. This statement completely defines the discovery and transformation through which I was about to journey. By the way, my novel still sits on my hard drive unpublished because I found a greater truth—a calling that had very little to do with being a novelist and everything to do with serving women as I do today.

Yes, Women's LifeLink, my online global community, was birthed from not only my desire to write but purpose, itself, prodding me to chase my passions and not dwell on my pain. And, starting a blog was all the rage at the time. Even with my newly found position as an administrator of a cool women's blog, I was still missing something: Authenticity.

I hid behind the digital pages of my website in fear that others would find out how dysfunctional my life really was. I atrophied in bed or at the ER much of the time—not exactly the life of a successful women's messenger. I would beat myself up daily for being inadequate, a fraud, for sometimes not even wanting to live. I entered the court of the guillotine.

But, facing this rock-bottom place meant there was nowhere else to go but up. The migraine disease wasn't just a condition; it had become an excuse to stay in my comfort zone. It just took me thousands of steps (and falls) on my self-development path to figure this out. My prayers had to change from being cries of "why me?" to determined intention to understand and accept what this season was teaching and to find the woman who was hiding in the shadows.

I will never forget the fierce moment when I escaped from the "guillotine" for good. It truly was a do or die decision that changed my life. First, I took an inventory of all that I'd experienced and surrounded each circumstance with clarity of purpose.

I saw patterns never seen before as a victim. I wrote down every lesson I'd learned to date; there were many. I then bathed my body with a loving intention and energy meditation. The next step came to me in a powerful instant of self-empowerment!

I walked to the bathroom mirror, stared myself down, believing I had control for the first time in 12+ years. I said, "Kellie, I love you. Body, I love you. But, FUCK this!" (Yeah, it had to be a robust statement.) I drew the line and was done with that season, making it quite clear to my mind, body, spirit, and the Universe.

Hope and peace unfolded that day. Then, I waited. A week later, my daughter was researching headaches and seizures, when she came across information that discussed the links between gluten, dairy, coffee and neurological conditions, including chronic migraine. I'd known about gluten years before and had even written about it on my website, but I never eliminated it from my diet.

Well, because she had experienced some seizures and was willing to try the new eating plan, I decided to do it with her. I dropped wheat, dairy, and coffee completely from my diet and immediately saw results! After the caffeine withdrawal headache ended two days later, the chronic migraine stopped. "Are you freaking kidding me?" All that time I suffered and it was just a silly food intolerance. It took me a week to even be happy.

What really transpired was the moment when you get what you want and yet grieve for the time that you didn't have it. Another lesson. But I got over it. The power came like a lightning bolt and shattered the guillotine into a million pieces!

I realized that I had existed in a place where illness was my normal and had even liked it to some degree. Don't get me wrong, I had hurt badly, but I allowed myself to be defined by it and; therefore, I let it be a safe place to hide from the authentic me and her dreams. Before I could move on with my life in a positive way, I had to deeply accept that a part of me was actually happy getting attention as a sick woman—a shadow.

Looking back at my transformation and the escape from the guillotine's blade, I now see that all change, whether physical or emotional, comes when the mind accepts new beliefs and releases the old.

In my case, I created the belief that I possessed power over my situation and that I could alter the trajectory of my life at any time. What brought me out of the illness and my negative thinking seemed like two simple acts: rebellion in the mirror and a diet change but was actually a long journey that only climaxed there...like a good book!

Today, I am Fibromyalgia, Depression, and Chronic Migraine free and loving my journey as a passionate messenger to women more than I ever have! I ask you this, "What beautiful things would happen if you believed something different about yourself or a situation?"

Lisa Marie Rosati

Visionary and Intuitive Lisa Marie Rosati is a renowned Transformation Catalyst for women. She's the Creatrix of The Goddess Lifestyle Plan™ & Sugar Free Goddess Program For Women™ and co-author of the international best selling books – "Embracing Your Authentic Self" and "In Pursuit Of The Divine". Lisa empowers spiritual women around the world on how to magically create an abundant life they love.

YOUR first step to becoming a Modern Day Goddess is awakening YOUR Inner Goddess from her deep slumber and identifying what "things" please her ... then with that knowledge, you can coax her out to play more often in your life inviting in more pleasure, fun and feminine power! Discover Your Goddess Life Recipe inside the pages of this effective and magical workbook.
http://www.goddesslifestyleplan.com/goddess-life-recipe-free-gift-page-ew

"Look for the life lessons that are hidden inside your struggles. They are the metaphorical crumbs that will lead you to the next level of your spiritual evolution." ~ Lisa Marie Rosati

BEAUTY, STRUGGLE AND LIFE MAGIC
BY LISA MARIE ROSATI

Beauty is such an emotionally charged word for most women… and I say for good reason… have you opened a magazine or flipped on the TV lately? The media is completely beauty OBSESSED and it seems to focus on external beauty giving very little attention to internal beauty. So for that very reason, I decided to devote my entire chapter in this empowering book to answering the burning question: "What is beauty and how does it relate to personal struggle and life magic?"

There's a well-known quote that I have thought introspectively about for years - "Beauty is in the eye of the beholder." Not only is "beauty" a personal opinion, the existence of beauty is dependent upon the lens you choose to look at life through. If you choose to focus in on the flaws and shadows that inevitably exist, that is what you will see; flaws and shadows… and in contrast, if you choose to look for the beauty and light that also exists in all situations, beauty and light is what you will see.

It's all about perspective and what you choose to put your attention on. Shadow and light always co-exist; it's a package deal so dictates the Law of Polarity. Darkness (shadow) is simply the absence of illumination (light) and visa versa.

The challenge for most people comes into play when painful, bad or tragic crap happens… most would immediately question how beauty can exist with suffering?

Being a Mystic, I've been on a spiritual journey for most of my life and to be totally transparent and honest, each time I have evolved it was through pain, sadness or personal struggle.

The process is what I affectionately call "A Fire Walk" - the transformative, spiritual journey through one's personal fires to the wisdom of complete understanding and acceptance of the life lesson attempting to come through. In my younger years I wouldn't accept struggle. I would get totally stuck on WHY! Have you ever done that?

I would ask myself "Why is this was happening to me?" or "Why did that happen to me?"

I had the tendency to look at any given uncomfortable situation I was dealing with up close and personal until the blessed day I realized that I was looking for my answers in all the wrong places. You see, the Divine speaks symbolically not literally. Most of us get caught up in the minutiae of the situation; the he said, she said nonsense... and that's the incorrect place to put your focus.

Each struggle we encounter has a life lesson that is trying to come through and it is our job to see the bigger picture and not dissect and over analyze the tiny details.

What I know for sure is that life lessons are usually NOT fun experiences, however they are always helpful if you learn from them.

One of my favorite metaphors about this teaching is a story about an oyster and pearl. The oyster from one grain of annoying sand creates a beautiful, luminous pearl.

That little grain of sand irritates the oyster's insides and instead of shriveling up and dying, the oyster creates this beautiful masterpiece from it's suffering – the pearl. I invite you to think about how you can create beauty from the things in your life that irritate you? That's actually my first thought when faced with unfavorable circumstances… how can I transform this crap sandwich into something useful and perhaps even beautiful? I'm a solutions kind of gal and I invite you to think about embracing that approach too!

True beauty is having the ability to use the magical process of alchemy to transform struggle, pain or suffering into something healthy and helpful for your life and for the life of others via a ripple effect. Have you ever thrown a rock into a placid lake and seen the ripples that vibrate out from the point of connection between the rock and the water? That's a ripple effect and it has more power than you realize, a tiny little shift in YOU will reach far and wide.

That ripple blesses you, your loved ones and the world. Alchemy occurs in an instant, the second a full body decision is made to accept what is and work with the situation at hand (no matter how crappy it is) instead of fighting against it. I've seen it happen thousands of times, in my own life and in the lives of the women I mentor. When life feels hard, overwhelming or like you're paddling a canoe upstream, I urge you to take a look at what you might be resisting. Are you resisting change, forgiveness or acceptance?

True beauty is defined by the empowered, internal shifts that occur within a woman who is open to receive divine guidance and grace. A stunningly beautiful and powerful woman is a woman who uses alchemy and her personal magic to transform even the most abominable of situations. Crappy things happen to good people all the time… that is a fact of life. To expect fairness across the board in life because you're a "good person" is spiritually immature; life just does not work like that.

When I was younger, I used to get all hung up and stuck on the "I'm a good person, so why is this happening to me?" thing. Not only did that way of thinking keep me miserable for a prolonged period of time, it kept me stuck and my personal vibration low therefore blocking my ability to attract high vibrational people, places and things into my life!

What I know for sure is that the Divine is not punitive in any way, shape or form... The Divine is neutral. The struggles that come our way are present for reasons bigger than we can understand in the moment. But I promise you, if you can create some healthy space and take a bird's eye view of the situation your dealing with, you will feel more peace.

One of my core beliefs and teachings is "life is magic if you choose it to be"... the good, the not so good bad and the ugly... the whole enchilada! There is life magic all around you in every moment. Magical living is simply having the ability to see the magnificent shining through the mundane.

Some of my personal examples of life magic would be when one of my children laugh with abandon, or the moment I become present and deeply inhale a fragrant bloom, or the moment I truly taste the food swirling around in my mouth, or the moment I quiet my mind chatter and connect soul to soul with one of my beloveds.

In order to recognize life magic you must be completely present in the moment. Most women I work with live in the past or the future, it's a mindset epidemic really. My clients tend to spend their time worrying about the future and/or beating themselves up over perceived passed mistakes.

This toxic and all too common practice of having one foot in the past and one foot in the future dilutes personal power but that all changes for them once I teach them about life magic and how to wield it at will!

I empower spiritual women magically create an abundant life they love by discovering how to call back their personal power and then channel it in the direction of their desires and dreams – pretty fabulous eh?

True beauty comes from owning your truth, warts and all and success in beauty is living and embodying YOUR personal truth; whatever that is for you. Life can feel long and full of struggle but it doesn't need to be that way. You are here in Earth School to learn, to grow and to evolve. For me, embracing and accepting that fact was essential to living a happy and beauty filled life.

I lead a very soul fulfilling life. I wake up every morning curious about what wonderful things might come my way. I expect magic and miracles, because I know that you get in life what you expect. What do you expect my beautiful friend? Are you always in a state of anticipation for the other shoe to drop or are you excited and curious about what each day might bless you with?

In conclusion, I want you to know that life magic connects you with your magical self, that part of you that knows truth, believes in miracles and can lead you to the life you've always dreamed of having. Your magical self wants you to experience pleasure, fun and connection. Your magical self wants you to be present and have more flow, ease and divine grace. Isn't it time your tapped into your life magic?

Marianne Chalmers Talkovski

Marianne has a life-long connection to holistic health and beauty. She is a licensed acupuncturist and esthetician. She gently guides individuals towards transformational insights, including recognizing personal strengths and opportunities. Marianne is a compassionate listener with an enthusiastic kind spirit who is honored to hold space for her client's transformation.

Through Chinese Face Reading, her clients repeatedly state that they truly feel special. If you would like to schedule a reading with Marianne to gain personal insights on the story of your life, you make book with her at www.shiningshen.com or become a fan on Facebook at www.facebook.com/LetUrShenShine.

LOVE YOUR WRINKLES, LOVE YOUR FACE BY MARIANNE CHALMERS TALKOVSKI

How do you define fulfillment or happiness? However you define it, it takes self-love to experience both. Self-love is the path to all healing. When you love yourself, you take care of yourself. Your family, friends, coworkers, clients and even strangers benefit from the light and love that radiates from you. So what is the secret to effortless fulfillment and happiness? The answer is self-love. This may sound cliché; however, I am going to briefly share with you an ancient wisdom that will help you view yourself in a different light as you navigate through life. I am going to teach you to love your wrinkles and love your face!

What if I told you there is a natural way to smooth and soften your wrinkles and to glow from within? My goal is to give you transformational insights that will inspire you to love your wrinkles and face so that you can feel beautiful and confident by embracing your inner beauty.

Why is this important? In other cultures, aging is an honorable process. Elders are revered with the utmost respect. However, in Western culture, we are often taught to criticize our features and wrinkles, while investing in extreme measures to stop the aging process. We inject toxins and chemicals into our faces to maintain a youthful appearance. We invest in chemical peels and embrace other harmful practices that promise to resurface our skin. I want to help you understand why you chose to stop a wrinkle from forming in a particular area and challenge you to think about your habitual expressions, and, if necessary, do the work to transform them from the inside.

As a holistic practitioner, I emphasize the importance of practicing self-care for your body, mind and spirit, which includes proper nutrition, the use of quality products, exercise, breath-work, and spiritual practices that will benefit your skin in its entirety. For now, let's focus on what each of your features represent.

Have you ever wondered why some people wrinkle differently than others? Chinese Face Reading is a science that branches from the ancient wisdom of Chinese Medicine and unlocks the story behind our facial features and wrinkle patterns. Chinese Face Reading gives us insight into our thoughts, behaviors, and personality, as well as the lessons we have to learn and where we are headed in life.

The face is a map that tells us what we have experienced in life and where we are getting stuck with particular issues. The face is the most dynamically expressive part of our bodies, and it is our emotional patterns that carve its landscape. When we understand the patterns that define our most common facial expressions, we can shift our attitudes and allow our inner radiance, or Shen, (as Chinese Medicine defines it), to shine.

Each feature on the facial map reveals something uniquely special, which corresponds to the energy of the seasons, or what we call the 5 Elements. When we flow with these seasons, we experience interconnectedness and non-resistance both in our lives and in our connection to nature because this is a brief overview.

We won't go in depth on the 5 Elements, but just know that our features and wrinkles can represent one to three meanings: an emotional pattern, a physical issue, or a significant life experience at a particular time in our lives. Let's discover more about our most expressive features and affirmations to transform potential negative thought patterns:

The FOREHEAD illustrates our experiences early in life, especially the many lessons we have learned before our 30s. When we experience something unexpected, we raise our eyebrows in surprise, confusion or even skepticism. This creates lines across the forehead that shows how intensely we've experienced life's twists and turns. To help us through these times we can affirm, "I flow with life easily and effortlessly."

The EYEBROWS are the area on the face where we express a vision for our future and new ideas. This is also the area where we indicate our ability to make and execute decisions and plans. When energy gets stuck in our eyebrows, it is often because we have been exerting strong emotional control or stressing over problem-solving, which leads to holding tension in this area. We show anger, frustration, skepticism, and intense concentration by drawing our brows together.

When there are lines between our eyebrows, it can signify that we are resistant to new ideas or have issues with authority. By relaxing this area consciously, we release our need to force an outcome. Inviting compassion and forgiveness into our hearts and mind allows us to soften these lines and to relax our eyebrows. We can consciously choose to affirm: "I choose to be open-hearted and compassionate. I am thankful for the growth that comes from forgiveness."

The EYES show how open our hearts are. When we are hurt or suspicious, our eyes become tense or narrow. When we consciously relax our eyes, we also relax our hearts. An open heart requires security and trust without self-judgment: "I choose love, joy and freedom and open my heart to allow wonderful things to flow into my life."

Some lines on the face are expected, including the lines surrounding the eyes that you may know as "crow's feet." In Chinese Face Reading, these lines are called Joy Lines. They indicate how much you enjoy life and how much people enjoy your company. The light from the eyes reflects the radiance of your heart or Shen. The healthier and happier we are, the clearer our Shen is.

In our culture, we are taught to be concerned about puffiness, dark circles or lines UNDER THE EYES. In Chinese Face Reading, these signs indicate unshed tears. When tears are unshed, there are feelings that we still need to feel or process. It is important to note whether these signs have been present throughout a person's life or whether they have appeared at a certain time. If unshed tears have appeared recently, it is important to grieve and let go.

The NOSE represents an exchange; it is where we take in air through inhalation and then find release through exhalation. This is a natural rhythm of life. When we feel stressed or overwhelmed, our breath becomes shallow. We absorb criticism but cannot release it.

The CHEEKS reflect our contentment and sense of safety, the sense of abundance in our lives. When we soften our cheeks, we release tension and free ourselves from unease that constricts us and prevents us from receiving all that we deserve.

A great practice for processing grief is to invite gratitude into our hearts, which helps us to accept and let go of unspent emotions. Receiving and releasing are one of the most important rhythms of our life: "I am grateful for everything I have and receive every day, including the lessons life teaches me. I let go of what no longer serves me."

Other features that are meant to appear on our face are the lines that run from the outside of the nose to the outside corner of the mouth. These are known as Purpose Lines and show how close we are to living our purpose; they should start to form by the time we reach our 50s.

The MOUTH is the area that depicts nourishment, generosity, receptivity, and enjoyment of indulgences. When we are disappointed or feel betrayed, we tighten our mouths, especially when those disappointments involve the past.

We create negative stories in our minds that affect our facial architecture. When we tense our mouths, we become martyrs unable to receive, and lines begin to form around our mouths.

Bad experiences, especially those caused by past relationships can affect our current or future situations. This is why it is so crucial to change our thought patterns, soften our mouths, and allow for the possibility of new experiences: "I am a generous person and enjoy sharing what I have. Receiving is also an act of generosity".

The CHIN reflects willpower, tenacity, determination and stubbornness; it represents a deep reserve of energy that helps us to withstand tough times. A wrinkled chin suggests that we have been working too hard or feeling extreme stress. We must relax and have faith: "I take time to rest, relax, and rejuvenate. I trust there are greater forces supporting me."

The JAW depicts our natural drive. When we are angry or over-exert ourselves, we tense our jaw and clench our teeth. This is the same energy expressed when our eyebrows are imbalanced. Practicing patience allows us to relax our jaws: "I am gentle, kind and patient with myself".

This is a brief overview of Chinese Face Reading. Through this fascinating area of study, we can understand the deeper meaning of our facial features and begin to respect our wrinkles and love our faces. Through this process of self-awareness, we can cultivate self-love, which is the path to all healing. Self-love leads to clear Shen. With clear Shen, fulfillment and happiness is effortless!

Michelle Elizabeth

Michelle Elizabeth is President and CEO of Effortless Extensions, as well as an American entrepreneur, marketer and inventor. Through her endeavors, Michelle Elizabeth is widely recognized as a charismatic pioneer revolutionizing and transforming each industry she works with. With over 30 worldwide patents, Michelle Elizabeth has received a number of honors and public recognition for her influence and motivational assistance to new and upcoming entrepreneurs.

As a mother of 5, grandmother of 10 and married to a retired Air Force Crew Chief, Michelle Elizabeth advocates and lives by "Shine as an Individual, Work as a team, Always Remember, Success unshared is Failure". http://www.effortlessextensions.com

BEAUTY: AN EFFORTLESS EXTENSION OF THE INNER YOU BY MICHELLE ELIZABETH

When I was young, I was very plain and frankly not a very pretty child. I grew up in the 60's and 70's, an era of long hair, bell bottom pants and Twiggy. Now for those of you not old enough to remember Twiggy, she was a tall beautiful model famous for her large eyes and very short hair (which I might add became know as the Twiggy hair cut). This extremely short hair became the newest fad, which I might add my mother thoroughly embraced, deeming it the perfect style for me. Now as it happens, on Twiggy it looked beautiful, on me...not so much! Now why would this be of any interest in this chapter, because "The Twiggy" would inadvertently become the path to my future success.

As I said I was not what you would call a pretty girl, and with the Twiggy style hair cut my mother so lovingly gave me herself (enough said), I looked like a boy. When the years passed and I was finally old enough to choose to let my hair grow out, I swore I would never have short hair again. I grew my hair long, yes the typical hippie hair that always seemed to hang in my eyes, I had the bell bottom jeans that hung on the ground, platform sneakers (yes, Platform sneakers) and the oversized military jacket that made my mother cringe!

Ok moving on, I spent the next few decades doing everything you could possibly do to ones hair! I highlighted, permed, frosted, dyed and bleached, then for good measure I made sure to use every heat styling tool known to woman that I could get my hands on. I made sure to do a really good job and over process my hair to the point that straw had a better texture than my hair. I had Bleach my hair blonde for one solid decade, and being naturally a dark brunette this was an every 3 to 4 week ritual to keep the roots at bay.

Now I had hair that was absolutely uncombable or brushable without tons of conditioner and then leave in conditioner. It was breaking at the rate of confetti falling at New Years Eve, and worse, would not grow.

The trip to my hairdresser, DUN DUN DA...... Total melt down! I was given the awful truth, I did this to myself, BUT it could be fixed! "I would need to go back to my natural color", ok I could do that "and cut off all the damaged hair to allow it to grow back"! Flash back, oh my gosh it was the Twiggy syndrome all over again!

Well it wasn't as bad as all that, but close, I did have to cut my hair fairly short but it was just below my ears and touching my shoulders. I was devastated; I couldn't bare to look in the mirror without feeling sick. I had grown out of the awkward stage when I was in my teens, mostly because of my long hair.

For me, I felt less...unattractive with long hair, it gave me my confidence, I was like Sampson, cut my hair, loose my strength. Silly I know, but we all have that "thing" that brings out our inner confidence, which in turn is our Effortless Extension of the inner beauty.

What does that mean exactly, an Effortless Extension of our inner beauty? Some of us have less confidence in ourselves because of our outer appearance, maybe its the shape of your nose, size of your ears, uneven skin....... we will all find faults in ourselves. The mirror can be a cruel judge, and the sentence of a lifetime, IF WE LET IT! But your Real Beauty lies under the surface, and when you are confidant it glows on the outside.

I had a hard time when I looked in the mirror after cutting off my hair, but as the saying goes "Necessity is the mother of invention" and because I couldn't find what I needed to make me feel confident in myself again, I invented it, in the form of Effortless Extensions. My new creation was named Effortless Extensions because of their ease of use, and the meaning behind it for me. I was able to feel confident again from the inside and that radiated on the outside.

My experience gave me insight into myself, and when I began to share that, first with my hairdresser, then the woman who became my business partner, I realized that what I had created could help other women feel more confident also. I have had women tell me they feel sexy and glamorous, that they have rekindled their intimate relationships because they do feel more confident.

It's amazing to me how something as simple as slipping on longer hair can give a woman an entirely new look, and with that a new sense of confidence. It's more than just slipping on hair, its slipping on the inner you. Taking hold and tapping into your inner beauty is something most of us lose when dealing with the daily chaos of life. As Mothers, wives, career woman etc, we sometimes forget to look, really look at the inner us. It's easy to throw on the sweat pants put your hair in a ponytail, and go about your day, telling yourself I don't have time to worry about what I look like. The reality is deep down you do care, and that is the reason you should take a few minutes each day to let your inner beauty out!

Example: I work from my home office, unless I have meetings to go to, no one sees me. I could walk around in pajamas, no make up, shower...don't shower...who cares? I DO! It's all about how I feel inside, and that comes through even if I am on the phone with someone. I want to be my best, feel my best, that doesn't mean I have to be dressed to the nines, it means confidence. I get up early, knowing my day starts at the same time as if I were punching the proverbial time clock. I get my shower, put on my makeup and slip on my Effortless Extensions. Why? because its my business and I want to feel confident when I talk about my product, and how it makes me feel.

As women we do want to feel sexy and desirable, that gives us confidence and even a sense of power. We need to feel that coming from within ourselves, it's finding what personally that is for each of us, but it IS there.

I have seen the transformation of many women over the years from just the simple act of slipping on an Effortless Extension. I have been told countless times how it has changed women's lives, and given them confidence, they actually hate having to take them off!

I never would have imagined that something that changed the course of my life, could have such a profound impact on so many women around the world. I have taken an idea that was meant to give me back my sense of confidence, and turned it into an international business, earning over 30 patents World Wide.

For me the greatest accomplishments still continue to be the individual experiences I am fortunate enough to be a part of. When I see the look of amazement on a woman's face when she tries on an Effortless Extensions for the first time! These may not seem like much in the reading of it, but it is in the living of it!

I'm not saying that my product is going to change anyones life, but it has made an impact on many women, and for that I am grateful! What I want every woman to take away from my experience, is knowing that Beauty is an Effortless Extension of the inner you, and its incumbent on each of us to find what it is that brings this out. Remember that "Beauty is in the eyes of the beholder" and when we see confidence in others we can see their inner beauty as well. It is inspiring, and purposeful, it is quietness and self esteem, it is understanding and self worth, it is loving ourselves enough to show the world that Our Beauty is an Effortless Extension of who we are inside.

Renee Dabney

Renee Dabney is the Inspirational Content Strategist and Message Muse. She is the owner of The Write Bud, which provides writing services for women business owners, speakers and coaches. Renee is committed to helping writers develop messages to share with their readers.

Renee has a corporate background in various fields from insurance companies to law firms. Renee holds an Associate's degree in Education from Community College of Philadelphia, a Bachelor's degree in English from Cornell University, and a Master's degree in English from Michigan State University. Renee has taught high school, college English courses, and privately tutored college students.

http://www.thewritebud.com
https://twitter.com/thewritebud
https://www.facebook.com/thewritebud
https://youtube.com/thewritebud
https://linkedin.com/thewritebud

THE ADVANTAGES OF ENHANCED BEAUTY: AN INTROSPECTIVE REALITY BY RENEE DABNEY

I went to the mirror and looked and looked and looked. I was terrified, avoiding it and thought about my past. The phrase "big nose" drummed in my ears. And the words "skinny" and "ugly" clouded my view. As a young adult I heard, "get it fixed!" A boyfriend even took me to a cosmetic surgeon.

But I forced myself to look again. I stood there and I kept looking, searching, seeking, and wondering. I was determined to find it. As I closely stared, her words deeply resonated loudly screeching like a halting freight train in my ears.

"What three qualities?" She said.

And after staring at myself for about ten minutes, I began to see them.

I then noticed that my three favorite facial features have a purpose and enhancing them is how I get to my greatness. Now the feelings I have about myself shows beautifully to others!

How I Got Here:

I won the Mother's Day Give Away Contest in May 2014 and part of the package of winning was a One hour Beauty Transformational session with **Charlotte Howard**, who is an Award-winning Hair Artist and Transformational Life Coach. The initial session included an audio CD with workbook titled *Creating a Beautiful, Sexy and Confident New You* along with a 30 minute follow-up session in 30 Days. During the first session, Charlotte asked me to find three attributes that I like about myself. These three features are what make me really feel beautiful and confident.

As a womanpreneur, I was super busy with an ever increasing daily-to-do list, and I started to neglect myself, so I felt the need to practice better self-care which helped me feel beautiful on the inside and out. And I knew that when I felt better about myself, I would have more confidence and I would reconnect with my dreams. The contest guidelines consisted of writing a 300-600 word essay on the challenges I faced with looking good and feeling beautiful from the inside out. I described my beauty struggles, and I explained why it's important for me to take action now to feel beautiful, sexy and confident.

After the follow-up session with Charlotte, my chapter was complete, and I knew I needed to participate in this anthology project. I not only figured out my favorite features, but I recognized the importance of enhancing my three features and how that enhancement could improve my life and spill into the lives of others. I know now that self-care is empowering.

The Beauty of Seeing With New Eyes:

I like the semi-oval and elongated shape of my eyes; my lashes are curly and give my eyes a feminine sensual look. I keep my eyebrows nicely trimmed, which frames my face and brings out the beauty of my eyes, which others notice. I accessorize my eyes with colorful eye shadows, eyeliner, and mascara by Maybelline, MAC or Motives.

Enhancing the beauty of my eyes:

I no longer focus on my outer physical attributes but more on the inner qualities. I see with a new perspective which is a positive point of view that shows others compassion and sincerity.

The Beauty of Speaking from My Lips:

My top and bottom lips are in symmetry with each other, meeting evenly in the middle and providing me with an attractive pout. I daily care for my lips with a moisturizing *lip conditioner,* and I exfoliate the top layer of skin with a sugar scrub and olive oil, which helps to keep them soft, eliminating dryness and chapping. I then make them more pronounced with a lip liner that matches my skin color, which I blend into my lips and then add attractive colored lip gloss during the day and a bright red or plum color for evening. My favorite products are MAC, Mary Kay and Motives.

Enhancing the beauty of my lips:

The words I speak from my lips have meaning. Words are everything and what people remember. So I speak pleasantly. My favorite positive affirmation is *(I am Super Fantastic),* which lifts my mood and energizes my spirit, and when encountering someone who looks like they need a lift, I will great them positively. I recognize that speaking pleasant words exudes power that conjures up great feelings that transpires into the lives of other people.

The Beauty of My Illuminating Smile:

My smile brightens my day and provides comfort and happiness to others. How I feel shows on my face through my smile. If my mouth is frowned or pursed, twisted and not relaxed, then people looking my direction will feel that I am not approachable, pleasant or open to their good nature. Also illuminating my smile is caring for my teeth by visiting a dentist every 6 months for x-rays and a professional cleaning and fluoride treatment and polish. I also brush and floss twice a day and in between meals whenever possible. I use Colgate tartar and cavity protection toothpaste.

Enhancing the beauty of my smile:

By just smiling daily, I increase my confidence, which leads to high self-esteem and self-worth and an increase in my happiness. My happy feeling go out and illuminate someone's day and makes them feel better. Smiling is an enormous energy booster.

My Beauty Challenges:

Previously, my beauty challenge has been the lack of focus on improving and maintaining my mental and physical self. I've always been an avid exerciser, but with a busy life, I began to lack the time needed to exercise. I knew early about the benefits of exercising, and I really liked the toned look of my arm, legs, and abdominals, and I enjoyed the spurts of energy and overall good feeling brought on by the endorphins created through a consistent exercise regimen. When time permitted, I did about an hour three days a week to include thirty minutes of cardio and thirty minutes of free weights.

During my extreme stress times and recent bout with severe depression, I learned about the benefits of meditation and yoga. I participated in the Oprah & Deepak 21-day Meditation Experience. It took some time to get my breath in rhythmic pattern and in synch with the stillness of my thoughts. Once I learned how to breathe deeply and quiet my mind's chatter, I understood and recognized the benefits of meditation and began to experience less stress and emotional discomfort. Yoga gave me more agility and flexibility, adding to my overall physical stamina and energy.

Overcoming My Challenges:

Currently, I work with a health coach, Shama Jenell of shamajenell.com, who directs me to use empowering words incorporated with subconscious mind training and to follow a healthy eating regimen. *Her Pamper Me Skinny and Health Equals Wealth* programs are phenomenal in lifting my spirits and realizing the areas of my life that need improvement.

She is my guidance and support, and she keeps me on track to achieve my mental and physical goals.

Also of interest are chakras, which are six energy points in the body that when activated increase the energy flow throughout the body. Each chakra represents a different level of consciousness, and when they are blocked an imbalance in the body results, so removing blocked chakras are important and allows me to express myself fully, and this expression helps me prosper in my life and business. I am learning how to remove the blockages by first again focusing on meditation and repeating a mantra, which is one empowering word and then positioning my hand on the area where a particular chakra is located. Through this technique I begin to mentally and energetically awaken myself spiritually and feel better.

A Beautiful Success:

The overall importance of maintaining a physical and mental health regimen is that I now know when I am depleted in spirit and my overall self-esteem and energy is lessened, and then I am not able to achieve any goals in life. I am also no good to anyone else, and my physical appearance begins to show the lack of focus on myself. Appearance is important for a business owner, because the first look is how clients and the public will perceive me, and I have to represent my brand professionally. When I am completely whole, I feel confident in my abilities, and my beautiful self-shows through, in not only how I look physically, but also how I serve clients, by successfully helping them achieve their desired results, which also positions me as a knowledgeable expert in the industry. When I look and feel beautiful, I naturally exert my sensuality that boosts my confidence as a woman in business, which is an attribute that is recognized and noticed when networking in public and also makes me very attractive, and therefore increasing the flow of my creativity and progression of business adventures and the overall improvement of my life.

Sirena Pellarolo

Dr. Sirena Pellarolo is a Midlife Midwife and Holistic Healer. She supports women in their menopause years to recover their juiciness and dive full-on into a vibrantly healthy and fulfilled second half of their lives. Specializing in weight management through life-changing programs that include DIY detoxifications, live foods and powerful transformational techniques, Sirena models for her clients how to courageously step center-stage in their lives by unleashing their unique personal power, creative self-expression and overall well being. Her approach? Going back to the basics of a healthy lifestyle: a personalized nutrient-rich diet, energizing physical movement and a meaningful spiritual practice.

www.sirenapellarolo.com
https://twitter.com/VivaSirena
https://www.youtube.com/user/pellarolo

MIDLIFE BEAUTY: THE REAL THING
BY SIRENA PELLAROLO

Last Sunday I participated in the Los Angeles Bridal Expo with a booth to promote my new six week intensive program targeted to mothers of the brides and grooms, "Glow and Look Radiant on Your Daughter/Son's Wedding."

To illustrate the cards that described the program, I used two pictures taken at my daughter's wedding, seven months ago. On the front I used this beautiful photo of my daughter in her wedding dress, stunningly foregrounding the image, and smiling, satisfied in the background, I, garbed with a beautiful lilac dress. In the reverse, I used a photo of myself as the mother of the bride, proud and elegant, a photo that I had used as my Facebook profile and had received over 200 likes. For the day of the Bridal Expo my attire was the same dress I wore for the wedding, as a clear sign of identification with all the mothers of the brides who visited the Expo.

Many attendees showed a true interest in my program and were glad to see that there was someone who addressed the plight of the mothers on that special day. I had several of them sign up for a Discovery Session as an initial health consultation with me, and I left the Expo happy and satisfied that I had followed my intuition and offered these services in such a venue. When I got home, I checked my Facebook page, and the posting of the program I had done in the morning had received 310 viewers!

I am telling this exemplary story of **success in beauty** because it is the culmination of several months--almost a year --, of a full personal and professional transformation. This journey led me to embody the **Midlife Midwife** who models for her clients how to courageously step center-stage in their lives by unleashing their unique personal power, creative self-expression and overall well-being.

My mission as a **Midlife Midwife** is to show by example how transformation is attainable for **Midlife women**; that it is possible to recover our juiciness and stay healthy, vibrant and beautiful after our reproductive years. And in fact, live a productive and fulfilled second half of our lives on our own terms now!

Here's the story. When my younger daughter Violeta announced her engagement with her boyfriend Andrew via a Facebook picture of the ring she received from him (that's how *I* found out, as I was vacationing in Costa Rica when the proposal happened), they decided to get married right away. Or at least, that's what I felt, as they gave us only nine months to prepare. I was thrilled with the idea of adding to my role as a mother the one as a mother in law, and eventually, a grandmother (which I will be, by the way, in a couple of months!), and was happy about their decision. However, as I looked at myself in the mirror, I realized I had some weight to release, and that I would do whatever I could to look beautiful and vibrant as the mother of the bride, step up to the occasion and make my daughter happy. I never knew then where this journey was going to take me.

You see? I retired early from my position as a tenured professor at 55 to pursue my passion of supporting individuals to use food as medicine as a preventative health option and live dynamic and happy lives. I became certified as a Holistic Health Coach and I offered programs that inspired my clients to reconnect with their bodies, minds and spirits by going back to the basics of a healthy lifestyle: a personalized nutrient-rich diet, energizing physical movement and a meaningful spiritual practice.

As a health coach, my approach to weight loss or the jump-starting of a healthy way of eating is a result of my own experience dealing with issues of weight management. Basically, to "crowd out" the unhealthy choices with nutrient-dense foods, mainly in the form of green veggie juices, smoothies and raw soups. I have found that many of my clients make astounding changes in their health by just adding these delicious drinks to their diets.

As their bodies start receiving their quota of intelligent nutrients, their cellular memory wakes up after a slumber induced by chemical-loaded, processed food and other addictive substances and the cravings shift towards the fuel meant to make our bodies operate in an optimal fashion: fresh, vibrant, locally grown veggies and fruits. Slowly but surely, cravings for non-supportive choices start melting away, as the body begins to crave natural, whole, clean foods.

Interestingly, I had been practicing this approach with my clients successfully for several years, but I had omitted to confess to them that my interest in healthy eating derived from my own history of eating disorders. I had been hiding behind my "expertise and authority'" as a coach, and had failed to share my own story.

The process of releasing weight for my daughter's wedding and becoming clear of many of the emotional issues that had kept the weight on, helped me come out of the closet with a part of myself I had been hiding and ashamed of for YEARS! I finally started to share my life story about the struggle with my body image. I realized that, if I wanted to grow as an individual and a professional, a necessary part of this growth process was to become honest in public.

This was very new to me. I usually don't talk about myself, as I'm generally the one who is lending her ear to those who need to talk. But opening up was part of my own healing process. As I acknowledged publicly my own journey, I became a mirror for those who travel similar paths, reflecting back to them the face of a fellow traveler. I hope these words communicate and inspire a message of radical self-acceptance, while illustrating how rejecting a part of ourselves can keep us from embodying our fullest potential, and how the "extra weight" we are carrying around may be compensating for those lost parts.

As a young woman growing up in Argentina, an image-obsessed country, I received messages early on about the importance of being beautiful, and that meant THIN. As I felt called to explore a much deeper experience of life, this inner struggle manifested as self-hatred and emotional eating. Consequently, I developed a very conflictive relationship with my body that resulted in serious issues of body image.

Part of the time I went along with the requirements of my culture; a better part of the time I was depressed and overweight. My story is about fighting my own truth my entire life: the fact that I was not naturally stick thin (the reality of MOST women) and did everything possible to achieve that ideal. When I did, it was short-lived and didn't provide the fulfillment I was looking for.

As I matured into my menopause years, my journey became one of self-acceptance and self-love: no longer punishing and rejecting myself to look or feel good "in the future," but with a deep desire to feel good and radiate this feel good energy in the present moment. My lifelong spiritual practices helped me achieve mental and emotional mastery.

I also learned that reestablishing a healthy relationship with food was the main contributor to re-awakening this feeling of wellness that was asleep in me. Eating certain foods fostered a vibrancy within that I was never able to access when I simply had restrictive or binge/purge diets. The releasing of a pattern that did not support my health activated my need to self-express through movement: I celebrate my body now, as I move it gracefully when I dance, when I swim, when I practice yoga.

My over five decades of experiencing a roller coaster relationship with my body have taught me a lasting and truly fulfilling way to thrive as my truest self from the inside out. I discovered the healing properties of food in its most natural state, and cultivated a newfound connection to the natural world around me. I learned how to satisfy my cravings for delicious food while providing nurturance to my body.

I was blessed to be my own guide through the process, learning through a bumpy path of trial and error. However, this self-initiated transformation has allowed me to gain the knowledge, strength and experience to guide other women through the journey back to body vitality in the gentlest, most effective way possible.

Just as the quest to discover my truest self was unique, so was the lifestyle and diet that I found to best suit me. I use this same approach with my clients, providing the support to find their own unique WHY behind the weight loss goal, and guiding them through creating a custom-designed diet suitable for their unique physical, emotional and spiritual needs.

Today, I look at the old beautiful pictures of myself as a young woman with a holistic understanding of what was going on with me "behind the scenes" during those years. I now channel the energy saved from romanticizing an imaginary beauty that can never be re-gained, towards envisioning, embodying and radiating my true self and ideal life right here and now!

You can do it too, and it is my honor to guide you in the empowering journey of releasing "what could have been," in exchange for embracing "what can be" and is possible still. I promise it's not too late!

Tina Hobson

Tina A. Hobson has been in the helping profession for almost 25 years, working as a Licensed Social Worker in the State of Ohio. Ms. Hobson received her BA in Social Work from Capital University in Columbus Ohio. Ms. Hobson has managed many social service programs including those associated with The State of Ohio and Cuyahoga County Alcohol, Drug and Mental Health Services.

As a member of The Word Church, Cleveland OH, Tina served as a Youth Court Social Worker where she facilitated a Faith-based program addressing youth issues. She also served as Juvenile Court advocate for troubled youth including but inclusive of facilitating crisis intervention.

Skype:
Iamasuperwoman2
216.406.3412
http://iamasuperwoman2.wix.com/iamasuperwoman2
https://www.facebook.com/tinaahobson
You are invited to Tina's monthly Blog Talk Radio Show (Last Friday of each Month 9pm EST)
http://www.blogtalkradio.com/iamasuperwoman2
Call in: 845.277.9243

STAYING INSPIRED WHEN FACING CHALLENGES
BY TINA HOBSON BSW, LSW

Over the past 61 years I've lived many lives. I have lived the life of selfishness and self centeredness. I have lived a life of self pity feeling that I was being done wrong and offended by others.

Yes, the root of most of my problems was just that, selfishness and self-centeredness. Thinking and feeling that the world owed me something. Believing that I should be the center of attention because poor me, I was black, poor me because I was skinny, poor me because my mother kept my brother and sent me to live with relatives hundreds of miles away.

Poor me because children called me a bastard because I didn't have a father in my life. Poor little me because my aunt died when I was 12 years old, how dare she leave me when she knew she was all I had to hold on to, to believe in, to cry to, to love, and to be there for me when I needed her, how dare she leave me. Poor me, poor me, poor me.

My life as I remember it as a little girl was full of negative thinking and perceptions. Through the progress of my life and trials these thoughts and perceptions caused many challenges and the motivators usually were not positive ones.

It was in the winter of 1966 I declared to God that since I am hurt, you don't love me, no one else loves me, I will do this thing called "life" on my own terms. This declaration led to my paying a high price to live a low life.

I lived the life of a drug addict with all of the personalities and behaviors that went along with those addictions to everything from alcohol, heroin, pills, marijuana to crack cocaine.

However, at the end of the day, I the poem "Footprints In The Sand" comes to mind "... He whispered, "My precious child, I love you and will never leave you never, ever, during your trials and testing. When you saw only one set of footprints, It was then that I carried you."

Staying inspired had a totally different meaning then that it has for me now. Today,I stay inspired by the Word of God to get me through any and all Challenges that I might face. My inspiration and motivation then was the instant gratification and excitement I anticipated when I ducked into that strange building to meet that stranger who had the drugs that I needed to mask that emotional, mental, spiritual and sometimes physical pain that I was feeling.

Being numb was my goal. It was in the stupor of numbness that not feeling was the best feeling I ever experienced. Then, the only challenges that I thought I faced was being attacked and robbed of my money or buying counterfeit drugs. Not once did I look at the long term affects of my behaviors, not even when I was robbed, raped, human trafficked, beaten, or left for dead. My goal was still to get high.

However, my best life is the life that I am living right now, a life full of love, vision, direction, energy and purpose. Due to some subliminal messages and some not so subliminal in my face messages, November 1, 1989 I sought help for my addiction and was admitted into the Psych ward of a local hospital and from there I was whisked into a residential addictions treatment program.

Those 120 or so days challenged me to the max; I was so confused, afraid and insecure. I wasn't sure I could do this thing called sobriety. I was scared!! What comes to my mind is Philippians 4:13 I can do all things through Him who strengthens me.

At the end of the day I know without a shadow of a doubt that I can do nothing of my own power. It has been tried and proven that each time in life that I have attempted to do things my way, guess what, those things were messed up completely.

When this student became ready, the teacher appeared. What a glorious day as I sat in that hospital that I surrendered my will and life over to the care of God. What a relief I didn't have to be afraid anyone.

It's been by the Grace of God that throughout my road of deliverance from addiction that I have been on a Mission to help others. That is why I am here writing right now, I was sent to tell you that no matter how far down the scale you have gone, you can GET UP! I was born for such a time like this, a time where my past and my present can make an impact on the lives of hundreds, thousands, even millions who don't think they have what it takes to live a peaceful life by telling my story.

I am here to tell you that what inspires me today is knowing that I can encourage others who have gone down similar paths as mine. I know that my story will give hope to the hopeless, power to the powerless and friendship to the friendless. I have to remember daily that God never left me nor was I forsaken. What I realized was that I had come to a time in my life where I had to be knocked down in order to get back up.

I've come a long way from drug addiction, immorality, prostitution, child abandonment, incarceration, suicidal ideations and attempts, but only by the grace of god. Where I was homeless I have been a home owner. Where I lacked a high school education I now have a bachelor's degree and a professional license. Where I became unemployed I am now a business owner. Where no one wanted to talk to me unless I had the dope including my last late husband who would sometimes brutally beat me beyond recognition when I would try to speak up for myself, to date I have spoken to rooms of hundreds of people sharing my testimony and hopefully saving lives.

I guess you are asking by now how I stay inspired when facing day to day challenges. Well let me tell you that my greatest challenge has always been and still is my thinking. I have come to realize that there is no other enemy in my life as threatening as me.

On a daily basis I fight the battle of my own mind. Proverbs 23:7King James Version (KJV) "For as he thinketh in his heart, so is he..." But know that there is a solution. My solution is staying focused. On a daily basis I must stay focused on what is happening in my life now and my future.

One of the tools that I use is my Vision Boards. I use my boards to remind me of the person that I have become and not to dwell on the person that I used to be. I use my Vision boards as a tool to move forward, knowing that I don't have to do anything alone but that I have a Creator that is with me every step of the way. My 2014 Vision Board is two sided. The one side is what I named "The God" side, it is here where I vision how God is working in my life and the things I have to do to continue on my Spiritual journey.

Helping, serving, empowering and inspiring others is the path that has been given to me to take. The word "Invest" is on my board and it means so much to me. It is so important that I invest wisely in every aspect of my life, spiritually, emotionally, physically, financially, and in time management. You see, that with Vision comes an assignment that must be fulfilled and my assignment is to work hard with tenacity to be the best person I can possibly be. My assignment is to be an example of an A.A. Promise which says: *no matter how far down the scale we have gone, we will see how our experience can benefit others.*

The other side of my board is the material things that I have visioned that I can have, but only when I appreciate and live the Spiritual side. Psalm 37:4 Delight yourself in the LORD; And He will give you the desires of your heart.

Having Purpose is so important; walking in my Purpose is even more significant. Now let's look at the definition of Purpose according to Dictionary.com… The reason why something is done or used; the aim or intention of something; the feeling of being determined to do or achieve something; the aim or goal of a person; what a person is trying to do or become, etc.

When I took a good look at that definition I began to smile because I was able to see myself through Spiritual lenses where before my lenses were clouded with self pity, self doubt and fear.

Scripture tells me that Psalm 139:13-14 "For You formed my inward parts; You wove (created) me in my mother's womb. 14 I will give thanks to you, for I am fearfully and wonderfully made; Wonderful are your works, and my soul knows it very well"

Through these spiritual lenses I began to see the reason for who I was, why I was, why I went through what I went through and why I am where I am today.

There are a lot of things that keep me inspired when facing challenges. When a test arises God always makes a way for me to meet any challenge I may face. His Word is and will always be my major and first source of strength. It is in His Word that I find solace and peace in the midst of the storm.

It is my hope and prayer that I have said something to inspire you to keep going and press through the challenges of life. I keep in mind that my past is in no way an indicator of my present and my future.

Know that you are not alone and that your peace in the midst of the storm is just a prayer away.

CONCLUSION

Are you ready to create what YOU want in life?

Then close your eyes and imagine that you are in a beautiful air balloon ready to take off, to have what you desire in your life. Now look toward the ground and notice if there are any ropes holding you down, stopping you from being free to fly. In order to go on in your life, it is necessary to cut those ropes--to overcome not your fears of failure but your fears of success. You may be as stormed as I was when I first noticed the fear of success during my personal, business and life journey.

It looks unreasonable to push aside the very things we want. We are unique, but our problems are not. See if you tear apart any of your fears, your blocks to success, YOU can defeat them and feel the exhilaration of flying free in your air balloon.

"Top Seven Fears YOU Shouldn't Have If YOU Want To Succeed at Pursuing Your Personal, Business and Life Journeys":

   1. **Fear of the unidentified**. "I don't know what it would be like to create what I want in life."

   2. **Fear that success doesn't fit your self image**. "What's an average girl from a small town doing hosting a radio show?"

   3. **Fear that people will not like you if you are successful**. "If I'm successful in my career, no man will desire me."

   4. **Fear that you don't merit success**. "I feel guilty because I once stole money from my parents."

   5. **Fear that success has a scary consequence**. "If I get the advancement, I won't have enough time to spend with my family."

   6. **Fear that your parents won't love you if you're more successful than they are**. "I don't want my father to feel bad."

   7. **Fear that to be successful is to fulfill your parents' wishes**. "I'm angry at them for not showing me enough attention when I was a kid. I'll show them--I won't have a successful career."

If you are ready to be all that you are and have what you desire, then close your eyes and imagine that you are in your beautiful air balloon. Feel the weights of the fears of success dropping off easily so that you can take off. Look below and notice the beautiful green meadow, the majestic mountains in the distance, and the peaceful blue sky filled with puffy white clouds. Notice that you are free to fly!

Are you ready to pursue a life of passion, master a positive mindset and achieve ultimate success by nurturing your heart, your mind, your body - and create the life you love? Connect with Success In Beauty Coauthors by visiting www.SuccessInBeauty.net

PURPOSE, PASSIONS AND DREAMS

Have you ever dreamed of writing, compiling and publishing your very own book that will make a difference in the lives of other women, sharing your expertise with the ultimate goal of attracting high quality clients and customer effortlessly?

Have you been telling yourself, that it is too much time to plan and produce a profitable and meaningful book? Well, all of that is about to change. Charlotte Howard has created Heart Centered Women Publishing just for YOU. Charlotte and her team will empower you to write, compile and publish your very own book using her world class team.

This is a proven way for you to get your book published affordable, stress free and professionally. It's YOUR TURN now to have your own book published. Connect with Charlotte Howard - Heart Centered Women Publishing to empower you to make your own book dream come to life.

Become one of her newest International Best Selling Authors, visit www.TheHairArtistAssociation.org or call 803-414-2117. Compelling testimonials and portfolio available upon request.

Made in the USA
San Bernardino, CA
15 November 2014